FASCINATING FACTS

ABOUT

FAMOUS FICTION AUTHORS

—•— AND THE —•—
GREATEST NOVELS OF ALL TIME

THE BOOK LOVER'S GUIDE
TO LITERARY TRIVIA

BY DAVE ASTOR

Fascinating Facts About Famous Fiction Authors and the Greatest Novels of All Time

The Book Lover's Guide to Literary Trivia

Dave Astor

Published by DaveAstorWrites.com
ISBN 978-0692851487

*This book is dedicated to my wife Laurel
and my daughters Maggie and Maria—
avid readers all.*

TABLE OF CONTENTS

INTRODUCTION

D id you know that the phrase "keeping up with the Joneses" originally referred to the wealthy family in which novelist Edith Wharton (nee Jones) grew up? That Shakespeare and *Don Quixote* author Miguel de Cervantes died on almost the same day in 1616? That the 1950s "Cat in the Hat" character created by Dr. Seuss looks like a feline version of the Uncle Sam character drawn by that same writer for his 1940s editorial cartoons?

You'll find those and other "wow"-inducing nuggets in *Fascinating Facts About Famous Fiction Authors and the Greatest Novels of All Time*.

Two more informational nuggets include something Charlotte Brontë did to her sister Anne and what Alice Walker did *for* Zora Neale Hurston years after Hurston died. What did Charlotte and Alice do? Um … I'm not going to tell you *everything* in this introduction!

I found the fascinating facts for *Fascinating Facts* by reading many biographies of great writers after their novels and other works piqued my curiosity about their lives. I also tapped other sources—including scholarly introductions to novels, Internet sites devoted to specific writers, and my own personal encounters with authors. Then I distilled the most interesting material into what you're about to read.

It's no surprise that wonderful wordsmiths have interesting facts surrounding them, because famous authors often have to be pretty fascinating themselves to create the literature we respect and admire. It's one reason I love writing about books in my weekly DaveAstorOnLiterature.com blog (whose knowledgeable readers recommended some of the authors featured in *Fascinating Facts*).

Why do I read fiction, and why should fiction avoiders consider giving it a chance? Literature can send our minds to another time and place, allowing us to forget our lives and troubles for a few precious hours. It can educate us about history, open our minds, increase our empathy, make us think, give us things to converse about, and/or provide plenty of excitement along with the escapism.

As you escape into *Fascinating Facts*, you'll find that it's organized into more than a hundred short chapters—all of which include several compelling pieces of information. So be prepared for great trivia, anecdotes, oddities, coincidences, and even trivial anecdotes that are oddly coincidental.

What's not odd is that the facts you're about to read (feel free to quote them at parties!) are in chapters arranged alphabetically by the last names of some of the best writers who ever lived. That's "lived" in the past tense, because the people featured in this book are deceased—although various living authors are mentioned in passing.

Why just writers no longer with us? Well, given that there are so many excellent authors, living and dead, one has to set some parameters for a book. Not to mention, we already know the work of these authors has stood the test of time.

Bonus for readers of
Fascinating Facts!

Get ten more FREE mini-chapters with fascinating facts about ten
other famous authors. That's seven more mini-chapters than novelist
Alexandre Dumas had musketeers!
Download it here www.DaveAstorWrites.com/bonus

SAY IT AIN'T SO, JO

Children usually outlive their parents, but by only two days? Yes, *Little Women* author **Louisa May Alcott** (1832-1888) died less than forty-eight hours after her father passed away. (Shades of Carrie Fisher and Debbie Reynolds in late 2016.)

Bronson Alcott was a reformer, writer, and educator who often had trouble earning a living. But the New Englander was "rich" in famous friends such as Ralph Waldo Emerson, Margaret Fuller, Nathaniel Hawthorne, and Henry David Thoreau—all of whom, along with Bronson, provided instruction to the brilliant Louisa at various times.

The Alcott family's finances improved markedly after the semi-autobiographical, Jo March-starring *Little Women* became a bestseller in 1868, and the prolific Louisa went on to write approximately twenty more books before her death twenty years later.

She and Bronson were also born on the same day (November 29), with her father's birth year in 1799.

HIS CAREER HAD MANY
A *FOUNDATION*

S cience-fiction legend **Isaac Asimov** (1920-1992) is best known for writing and editing an astonishing 500-plus books, including the *Foundation* novels and the *I, Robot* short-story collection. But he also directly or indirectly made his mark in various other media.

For instance, the aforementioned story collection inspired the 1977 *I Robot* album from The Alan Parsons Project. Also, Asimov's fictional concept of "positronic" technology helped inspire the Lt. Data character in the 1987-1994 TV series *Star Trek: The Next Generation*. The android Data—played by actor Brent Spiner—had a "positronic brain."

And Asimov, who coined the word "robotics," made his presence felt in newspapers by writing a syndicated column during the latter part of his life. I attended the 1986 event in New York City announcing Asimov's Los Angeles Times Syndicate (LATS) feature, which, not surprisingly, focused on science. Asimov was friendly and approachable (and had impressive mutton-chop sideburns!).

Speaking of newspapers, Asimov's brother, Stanley, was an executive at *Newsday* and his nephew, Eric, has been affiliated with *The New York Times*. And Isaac's wife, Janet—a notable author in her own right—helped write the LATS column after her husband's health began to fail and then continued it after his 1992 death.

WHAT HAPPENED AFTER SHE STOPPED MAKING *SENSE*

When it came to publication and sales success, delayed gratification was **Jane Austen**'s fate.

Austen (1775-1817) wrote differently titled early versions of *Sense and Sensibility* and *Pride and Prejudice* in the 1790s, but those sublime books weren't published until 1811 and 1813, respectively.

Sales of Austen's novels—which also included *Emma*, *Mansfield Park*, and the posthumously released *Persuasion* and *Northanger Abbey*—were decent during her lifetime and soon after she died. But the author's work didn't explode in popularity among readers (and academics) until many decades later. One thing that helped was 1869's *A Memoir of Jane Austen* by her nephew, James Edward Austen-Leigh.

As for the 2009 parody novel *Pride and Prejudice and Zombies*? Probably best that Austen wasn't around to see the success of *that*. The titular *Emma* character Emma Woodhouse, who initially meddled in the love life of her friend Harriet, seemingly couldn't dissuade zombies from marrying an Austen novel.

ONE GREAT AUTHOR WHO EXPERIENCED TWO KINDS OF BIAS

Many authors have at least one semi-autobiographical novel in their writing quiver. Such was the case with **James Baldwin** (1924-1987) and his *Go Tell it on the Mountain* (1953).

Baldwin's stepfather was a preacher who treated him more harshly than his other children—which served as a model for the troubled relationship between John Grimes and his abusive stepfather, Gabriel, in Baldwin's riveting debut novel. The real-life James and the fictional John also shared youthful, temporary bouts of becoming more religious.

Something of Baldwin was also in *Giovanni's Room* (1956), one of the few novels to explore gay identity published before the modern gay rights movement. One way that book differed significantly from *Go Tell it on the* Mountain was its cast of mostly white characters.

Baldwin left the U.S. for Paris in his twenties to escape blatant racism and homophobia and to widen his horizons as a writer. He would end up spending a large part of his life in France—where he became fluent in the language and was visited by friends such as Josephine Baker, Harry Belafonte, Miles Davis, Sidney Poitier, and Nina Simone. The author, a civil rights activist for many years, also knew three iconic leaders—the Reverend Dr. Martin Luther King Jr., Malcolm X, and Medgar Evers—who ended up being assassinated.

THE SUCCESS OF AN AUTHOR GIVEN TO EXCESS

I t's not surprising that **Honoré de Balzac** (1799-1850) died relatively young after a lifetime of all-night writing marathons, little exercise, and endless cups of coffee. What *is* surprising, or at least sort of odd, is that the French author passed away in a year that combines the ages of his mother (eighteen) and father (fifty) when they married.

But what a career before Balzac's death! He wrote relentlessly— starting with forgettable potboilers published under pen names before maturing into the author of compelling novels such as *Old Goriot*, *Cousin Bette*, and *Eugenie Grandet* (one of his less sprawling books, and a gem). Much of this output was under the umbrella of "The Human Comedy," a series designed to depict various rungs of French society from 1815 on. The series contained more than ninety finished works (including novels and stories but not Balzac's plays) and forty-plus unfinished ones. The style was literary realism/ naturalism, and—as Emile Zola later did with his Rougon-Macquart novels—characters periodically appeared in more than one book.

Balzac's fiction would influence not only Zola but also Charles Dickens, Fyodor Dostoyevsky, Henry James, Marcel Proust, and various other authors.

Like many creative geniuses in a rote environment, Balzac didn't fit in and didn't do well at school. He was frequently sent to the school's "dungeon," but that gave him the opportunity to devour books.

HE PLEDGED ALLEGIANCE TO A UTOPIAN FUTURE

D id you know that **Edward Bellamy** (1850-1898) predicted debit cards in his 1888 book *Looking Backward*? That and many other things in the socialist-utopian novel put enthralled readers in Bellamy's debt.

Citizens in the Bellamy book's ideal fictional society were given a piece of pasteboard for a certain number of dollars. When they made a purchase, the clerk removed little squares corresponding to the value of what was ordered.

Looking Backward, set in Boston in the year 2000, was one of the best-selling books of the nineteenth century—along with novels such as Lew Wallace's *Ben-Hur* and Harriet Beecher Stowe's *Uncle Tom's Cabin*. Indeed, Bellamy's time-travel *tour de force* was so influential in its day that it inspired dozens of "Bellamy Clubs" that discussed and further publicized the author's ideas. *Looking Backward* also influenced legendary labor leader Eugene Debs to move in a more progressive direction.

Edward was the cousin of Francis Bellamy, creator of The Pledge of Allegiance—which, to the dismay of profit-obsessed banks, doesn't pledge allegiance to no-interest checking accounts tied to debit cards.

A MARRIAGE OF WRITING TALENT AND ... MARRIAGES

Here are some numbers for **Saul Bellow**: one Nobel Prize, one Pulitzer Prize, and one day too late (a young Bellow visited Mexico in 1940 to meet Leon Trotsky, but arrived the day after the exiled Russian revolutionary was assassinated).

And five marriages. Perhaps a record or near record for a major novelist? He even had his fourth child at the advanced age of eighty-four.

The Quebec-born Bellow (1915-2005) was the son of Russian immigrants who moved to Chicago when the future author was nine. He was a Trotskyist as a young man (hence that trip to Mexico) and later grew more conservative as he aged. But Bellow did teach at several "liberal" universities: Yale, NYU, Princeton, and elsewhere. And though sometimes accused of racism, he was a close friend of *Invisible Man* author Ralph Ellison.

Bellow's best-known novels—a number of them with a Chicago setting, a focus on Jewish life, and a sprawling, Dickensian flair—include *The Adventures of Augie March, Seize the Day, Henderson the Rain King, Herzog, Mr. Sammler's Planet,* and *Humboldt's Gift* (which won the author his aforementioned Pulitzer in 1976).

WHEN HE COULD STILL SEE, HE SPOTTED SOME COATS

A fter the mesmerizing Argentine short story writer **Jorge Luis Borges** (1899-1986) went completely blind in his later years, one person of great assistance to him was his mother, Leonor. As Borges notes in an autobiographical essay in the back of the 1970 collection *The Aleph and Other Stories*, Leonor did secretarial work for (and often traveled with) Jorge into her nineties.

But Leonor also made her own literary mark by translating the works of authors such as William Faulkner, Nathaniel Hawthorne, Herman Melville, and Virginia Woolf.

Before Borges became a renowned short story writer, he received some minor renown in the 1920s for a book of poems titled *Fervor de Buenos Aires*. One interesting way he distributed that book was having someone go to the cloakroom of the *Nosotros* literary magazine's office and put copies in the overcoat pockets hanging there.

"When I came back after a year's absence," Borges wrote in the aforementioned essay, "I found that some of the inhabitants of the overcoats had read my poems, and a few had even written about them."

Borges' fiction—which contains elements of philosophy, fantasy, and magic realism—influenced a later boom of superb Latin American writers whose numbers include Gabriel Garcia Marquez (*One Hundred Years of Solitude*) and Isabel Allende (*The House of the Spirits*).

FROM HARASSING SO-CALLED WITCHES TO THE BURNING OF BOOKS

Ray Bradbury (1920-2012) was a descendant of Mary Bradbury, who was tried and convicted at the infamous Salem witch trials of 1692. Perhaps that was one genetic strand leading Ray to become a sci-fi/fantasy writer with an often-spooky touch?

Indeed, Bradbury's most famous works—including the dystopian classic about book burning *Fahrenheit 451* as well as *The Martian Chronicles, The Illustrated Man*, and *Something Wicked This Way Comes*—have many disturbing elements. But the author was also capable of sunnier works, including the semi-autobiographical *Dandelion Wine* about one summer in the life of a boy growing up in the Green Town burg based on Bradbury's hometown of Waukegan, Illinois. Still, even as that novel fondly recalled a 1920s Midwest childhood, there was also death and other troubling events in its pages.

Bradbury had a hand in other media, too, writing the screenplay for the 1956 *Moby Dick* movie starring Gregory Peck as Captain Ahab, appearing on Groucho Marx's *You Bet Your Life* TV show that same year, seeing his short story "I Sing the Body Electric" become a *Twilight Zone* episode, hosting the syndicated TV series *The Ray*

Bradbury Theater, etc. His close friend Gene Roddenberry asked Bradbury to write for *Star Trek*, but that never happened; Bradbury, despite his experience adapting Herman Melville's whaling novel for the big screen, had trouble creating stories he didn't think up from scratch.

Bradbury was someone who took his readers everywhere, but he never learned to drive.

UNEXPECTED CAUTION AND CONVENTIONALITY

The only two books by **Anne Brontë** (1820-1849) included one good novel (*Agnes Grey*) and one great novel (*The Tenant of Wildfell Hall*), but her authorial fame pales compared to her sisters Emily (*Wuthering Heights*) and Charlotte (*Jane Eyre*). That was partly Charlotte's fault.

Charlotte loved her sister Anne, but prevented republication of *Wildfell Hall* after Anne's death. Was the book too shocking for its time (in its depiction of alcoholism)? Was it too feminist for that more patriarchal era (Helen leaves her debauched husband and supports herself and her son by painting)? Yet Charlotte allowed republication of Emily's dramatic, impassioned *Wuthering Heights*, and *Jane Eyre* was certainly feminist and groundbreaking in its way. Perhaps Charlotte wanted to cling to the idea that her youngest sister was more "innocent" than she was.

Anne spent several years working as a governess—a position also held by Agnes Grey and Jane Eyre. The *Agnes Grey* novel did modestly well, but the subsequent *Wildfell Hall* sold out in just a few weeks. Too bad Charlotte later sold out her sister in a way.

THE BELL NOT OF AMHERST

Emily Dickinson was posthumously known as The Belle of Amherst. **Charlotte Brontë** was a Bell of England.

When Brontë's *Jane Eyre* masterpiece was published in 1847, it bore the ambiguous but male-sounding pen name of Currer Bell. That's because it was much harder for a woman than a man to get published in the nineteenth century. Charlotte's sisters Emily Brontë and Anne Brontë also used pseudonyms: Ellis Bell and Acton Bell.

Another reason why an alias suited Charlotte was her aversion to publicity. But Charlotte's real name did come out, and the *Jane Eyre* author ended up meeting fellow famous novelists such as William Makepeace Thackeray (*Vanity Fair*). The shyness remained, however. Thackeray's daughter recalled Brontë (1816-1855) visiting her father's home and barely saying a word—though Brontë's intellect and passion were there for all to see in *Jane Eyre* as well as works such as *Villette*, a brooding novel written after the untimely deaths of Emily and Anne.

Brontë married her father's curate, Arthur Bell Nicholls (hmm … interesting middle name), less than a year before she died during pregnancy. Scholars feel Nicholls—who would live until 1906—might have been the partial model for *Jane Eyre*'s memorable Rochester and St. John. But, unlike Rochester, the curate did not have a first wife in the attic.

WUTHERING HEIGHTS AT THE HEIGHT OF THE POP CHARTS

Emily Brontë (1818-1848), who died young, inspired a young singer more than a century later.

Brontë's one novel, of course, is the legendary *Wuthering Heights*. That's also the name of a 1978 number-one hit written and sung by Britain's Kate Bush, who was nineteen at the time. Two "official" versions of the song are on YouTube, where Bush's singing and dancing have some of the spookiness and offbeat nature of Brontë's book.

Interestingly, Emily and Kate were each born on July 30—in Bush's case, in 1958.

Literary and author references are surprisingly numerous in rock and pop music, whether it be Led Zeppelin's "Ramble On" (which alludes to J.R.R. Tolkien's *The Lord of the Rings*), Jefferson Airplane's "White Rabbit" (Lewis Carroll's *Alice's Adventures in Wonderland*), Bruce Springsteen's "The Ghost of Tom Joad" (John Steinbeck's *The Grapes of Wrath*), The Roots' "Things Fall Apart" (Chinua Achebe's novel of the same name), 10,000 Maniacs' "Hey Jack Kerouac," Rosanne Cash's "The Summer I Read Colette," etc.

Like a number of novels later acknowledged as masterpieces, *Wuthering Heights* received mixed reviews when first published—with some critics and readers taken aback by its tempestuous content and the enigmatic Heathcliff's cruel personality (shaped by the cruelty

27

he suffered as a boy). The book was ahead of its nineteenth-century time in various ways, but certainly fit the zeitgeist of the twentieth-century when Kate Bush tackled it musically.

A "Laureate of American Lowlife"

Charles Bukowski (1920-1994) lived a life of many lows: son of an abusive father and then an adulthood of poverty, alcoholism, and more. But the highs were quite high.

Heck, the title of one of his poetry collections—*The Days Run Away Like Wild Horses Over the Hills*—was repeatedly quoted in the 1993 "Dirty Day" song by superstar rockers U2. And Bukowski wrote the screenplay for the well-received 1987 movie *Barfly*—an experience he fictionally recounted in his hilarious, roughly charming 1989 novel *Hollywood*.

That was one of six novels penned by Bukowski, who also wrote enough poetry to fill thirty-plus collections (some published posthumously). Then there were more than a dozen short-story collections (again, some released after the author's death), nonfiction books, and more. Most of Bukowski's major work was published by Black Sparrow Press, which took a chance on the initially almost-unknown writer and to which Bukowski remained loyal and grateful after he became more famous.

Bukowski's frequently semi-autobiographical work usually focused on the down-and-out—earning the author a *Time* magazine designation as a "laureate of American lowlife."

Born in Germany to a German mother and German-American father, Bukowski ended up spending much of his life in Los Angeles—but not the wealthy part of that city.

DEATH DID NOT ARRIVE LIKE *CLOCKWORK*

Did the 1962 novel *A Clockwork Orange* almost not exist? Its author, Anthony Burgess, collapsed in 1958 while teaching in Brunei and was told he had an inoperable brain tumor that would kill him within a year.

To provide money for his wife, Burgess wrote several novels during that year—but didn't die. In fact, there are doubts he had a brain tumor at all.

Of course, Burgess accomplished a lot more than writing *A Clockwork Orange*, which was turned into a 1971 movie more famous than the book. He wrote more than thirty novels, including the memorable *The Kingdom of the Wicked* chronicling the early years of Christianity and featuring characters such as a rather human Jesus Christ and the Roman emperor Nero. Yes, Rome burns in the novel, which ends with a certain lava eruption burying Pompeii in 79 AD.

Burgess (1917-1993) also wrote literary criticism, penned screenplays, became an expert in languages (real ones and those he created), and composed more than 250 musical works. His linguistic and musical interests were evidenced in *A Clockwork Orange*.

Also, the English-born author lived and worked in various countries—including the United States, Italy, and what is now Malaysia.

TRAUMATIC MEDICAL INTERLUDE FOR AN EARLY FEMALE NOVELIST

To call **Fanny Burney** (1752-1840) a woman ahead of her time would be a major understatement. She was a published novelist during an era when few of her gender managed that. And her frank written account of undergoing an 1811 mastectomy without the benefit of not-yet-invented anesthetics is riveting and harrowing.

One excerpt: "I began a scream that lasted unintermittingly [sic] during the whole time of the incision—& I almost marvel that rings not in my Ears still?"

But, if Burney indeed had breast cancer, the primitive operation succeeded in giving her nearly three decades more of life.

Burney wrote four novels—including *Evelina*, which had to be published anonymously because of her gender. Her comic take on the lives of the affluent, and her insight into the role of women in a patriarchal society, inspired later authors such as Jane Austen. Indeed, Austen may have taken the title of her iconic *Pride and Prejudice* from a line in Burney's *Cecilia* novel.

Though her books were popular, Burney's eight plays were hardly performed during her lifetime. She was also known for the extensive journals she wrote over a period of *seventy-two years*—from 1768 to 1840.

From 1786 to 1790, Burney worked in the court of George III and Queen Charlotte. The king, of course, was *not* ahead of his time when it came to how he treated the Thirteen Colonies.

A Sci-Fi Writer Who Broke the Mold

Who was the first science-fiction author to receive a MacArthur Fellowship? You have a few seconds to guess ... waiting ... time's up. It was **Octavia E. Butler**, who was awarded that lucrative "Genius Grant" in 1995—fourteen years after the fellowship began in 1981.

Butler (1947-2006) was also a pioneer in another way: an African-American woman writing in a literary genre dominated by white men. Her canon included fifteen novels, with perhaps the best-known being the best-selling *Kindred* (1979)—a riveting, searing time-travel tale of a black woman repeatedly yanked from twentieth-century California to slavery times in the American South.

Kindred was one of Butler's two standalone novels (along with *Fledgling*). She also wrote the *Patternist*, *Xenogenesis*, and *Parable* sci-fi series, which consisted of six, five, and two books, respectively.

The California-born Butler—whose fiction often had an antiracist, feminist, political, and sociological edge to go along with excellent storytelling—was the daughter of a housemaid and a shoeshine man. Her mother would give Octavia books and magazines her employers discarded, and the shy daughter also spent lots of time reading in the Pasadena Public Library, where she became hooked on sci-fi. She initially struggled to make a living in that field, but was eventually helped by noted sci-fi writer Harlan Ellison—and by her growing maturity as a writer.

Butler's MacArthur award was a very nice $295,000.

ITALO FROM ITALY
AND ELSEWHERE

I t almost goes without saying that many fiction writers create at least some characters much different than themselves.

For instance, *Marcovaldo* by **Italo Calvino** (1923-1985) stars an impoverished, at-times-bumbling dreamer with not much of an ideology other than a sort of restless curiosity. But the popular Italian author of that droll/depressing short-story-collection-as-novella came from an affluent family, made the courageous decision to join his country's anti-fascist resistance during World War II, and was a committed leftist for most of his remaining life.

Calvino (who did his master's thesis on author Joseph Conrad) was born in Cuba, where his Italian father was working at the time. He came full circle in a way after getting married in Cuba in 1964—even meeting Che Guevara during that wedding sojourn. He later lived in France and traveled to many other nations.

That was another difference between the author and the fictional Marcovaldo, who often wandered the industrial city where he lived but never left Italy.

SHADOWS ON THE ROCK KNOWN AS MANHATTAN

Willa **Cather** (1873-1947) mentions religious mass in *Death Comes for the Archbishop*, but mass transit was more problematic for her.

The Nebraska-raised Cather and her close friend (and life partner?) Edith Lewis lived in an apartment in New York City's Greenwich Village from 1913 to 1927 (the year *Death Comes for the Archbishop* came out). But they had to move when the building was scheduled to be demolished for a subway line.

During the first five of those fourteen years on Bank Street, Cather saw the publication of her acclaimed *Prairie Trilogy*: *O Pioneers!*, *The Song of the Lark*, and *My Antonia*. Subways did not figure in any of those books, as Manhattan's "N" train did not have a Nebraska station.

After her 1927 move, one of Cather's best late-career books was *Shadows on the Rock* (1931). The *Shadows* setting was the rock of Quebec City, not the Manhattan rock workers bored through for the subway line that cost Cather her apartment.

THE NEAR-DEATH EXPERIENCES OF TWO LITERARY LEGENDS

To be or not to be … tilting at the windmills of death within a day of each other.

Don Quixote author **Miguel de Cervantes** (1547-1616) and playwright/poet **William Shakespeare** (1564-1616) died on April 22 and April 23, respectively, with Cervantes being buried on April 23. But Shakespeare actually passed away ten days later.

How could that be? By 1616, Spain had adopted the Gregorian calendar, while England was still using the Julian calendar. So if England had also gone Gregorian at the time, Shakespeare would have died on May 3.

Either way, the almost-simultaneous passing of those two writers was nearly as coincidental as U.S. founding fathers John Adams and Thomas Jefferson both dying on July 4, 1826—the fiftieth anniversary of America's first Independence Day.

In conclusion, the Shakespeare sonnet line of "From you have I been absent in the spring" could have been slightly rewritten in 1616 to say *permanently* absent.

EDNA AND EROTICA AS AN AUTHOR PUSHED THE ENVELOPE

Some authors are too far ahead of their time to get the respect they deserve while alive to enjoy it.

Such was the case with **Kate Chopin** (1850-1904), whose novel *The Awakening* was considered scandalous when published in 1899. Why? Told by a female author from a female character's point of view, the book depicts the growing independence and sexual awakening of a woman stuck in the gilded cage of a marriage to a decent but conventional man. Edna Pontellier, who has two young sons, is also often indifferent to motherhood. The negative reaction of many readers and critics (including a young Willa Cather) basically put a halt to Chopin's writing career.

Edna, who became a feminist heroine to many when *The Awakening* was rediscovered numerous decades later, is indeed courageous in her way—and very smart, too. But tarnishing some of that luster is her rather spoiled nature and her (or perhaps Chopin's) casual superiority whenever African-American servants are mentioned. It's a shame when a person is enlightened in some ways but not in others. The fact that Chopin's family owned slaves during her youth may have had something to do with that.

Born in St. Louis, Chopin moved to New Orleans after marrying and eventually had five sons and a daughter before becoming widowed in her early thirties. Turning to writing, she penned three novels and nearly a hundred short stories from 1889 on. One tale, the erotic "The Storm," wasn't published until 1969. So *The Awakening* wasn't Chopin's only controversial work.

A FACTUAL MYSTERY INVOLVING A FICTIONAL MYSTERY WRITER

For someone who wrote dozens of enduring mysteries, the biggest **Agatha Christie** mystery may have involved herself. The English author (1890-1976) was already famous when she disappeared in 1926 after her husband Archibald asked for a divorce (he was in love with another woman). Agatha's car was found abandoned, reward money was offered, more than 1,000 police officers and about 15,000 volunteers searched for her, and Arthur Conan Doyle even gave a spirit medium one of Christie's gloves to aid in the hunt. Meanwhile, the disappearance was featured on the front page of *The New York Times*.

Christie was found in a hotel ten days later—possibly suffering from amnesia, or perhaps depressed about the divorce request, her husband's infidelity, the death of her mother, and/or overwork. During her life, she would write more than seventy novels and also pen short-story collections and plays.

The author—who remarried happily in 1930—had her greatest success with *And Then There Were None*. It has sold about 100 million copies, making it the most popular mystery of all time and one of the most popular novels of *any* kind. Overall, Christie is considered the best-selling novelist ever, with about two billion copies bought. And *The Mousetrap* play she wrote has been continuously running since 1952—more than 26,000 performances as of 2016.

Her best-known characters were Hercule Poirot and Miss Marple, but even those brilliant fictional sleuths couldn't find Christie when she disappeared.

A Career That Included *Shogun* and Show Biz

James Clavell (1921-1994) was an Australian-born Brit who moved to America in his early thirties, but Japan and the Japanese people played an important role in his life and writing career.

During his World War II military service, Clavell was captured and suffered greatly in a Japanese prison camp. Decades later, he wrote the long, riveting *Shogun* novel set in seventeenth-century Japan (the year 1600, to be exact). That best-selling 1975 book was turned into a highly rated 1980 miniseries starring Richard Chamberlain as English ship pilot John Blackthorne—who ends up in Japan, is taken prisoner (sound familiar?), learns Japanese, has near-death scrapes, has an affair with the memorable Mariko, and more.

Clavell wrote several other blockbuster novels—including *Noble House*—and was also well known for his movie work. For instance, he wrote *The Fly* (1958), co-wrote *The Great Escape* (1963), and wrote and directed *To Sir, with Love* (1967).

ALL FOR ONE, AND TWO FOR DIVERSITY

Was Gigi one of The Three Musketeers? Nope. But the very different French authors **Colette** (1873-1954) and **Alexandre Dumas** (1802-1870) did have one thing in common: partly black ancestry.

Dumas' dad, who served as an officer under Napoleon, was the half-black son of a Caribbean woman; his wife (Alexandre's mom) was white.

Alexandre—best known for his revenge epic *The Count of Monte Cristo* and his swashbuckling yarn *The Three Musketeers*—tended to ignore racial issues in his novels. But there was one major exception among his huge canon of books: 1843's *Georges*, which tackled prejudice amid a rousing adventure plot.

The also-prolific author Colette, whose maternal grandfather was partly black, mostly created quite-white characters in novels such as *Claudine at School*, *The Vagabond*, *Cheri*, *Break of Day*, and *Gigi*. The star of the last book inspired the Lerner and Loewe movie song that goes: "Gigi ... have I merely been too blind to realize" (that your creator was multiethnic).

Speaking of Colette, how's this for a coincidence? She was born on January 28 and died on August 3, and her third husband, Maurice Goudeket, was born on August 3 and died on January 28!

THE WOMAN IN WHITE AND THE WOMEN IN HIS LIFE

The close relationships of **Wilkie Collins** (1824-1889) included one high-profile one and two lower-profile ones. British readers were well aware that Charles Dickens and Wilkie Collins were close friends and that the older Dickens was a mentor to Collins. Wilkie's work appeared in Dickens' journals, he and Charles acted together in amateur productions, and Collins' younger brother (also a Charles) married one of Dickens' daughters.

Collins' lower-profile relationships were with two women—Caroline Graves and Mary Rudd—whom he lived with simultaneously in two different households (under an assumed name in one of those abodes).

Despite this unconventional and problematic arrangement, Collins was capable of creating strong, modern, almost "liberated" women in his fiction. Those characters included Marian Halcombe in the thrilling mystery *The Woman in White* and Lydia Gwilt in the compelling *Armadale*, which features characters who share the same name.

Collins is also famous for *The Moonstone*, one of the first detective novels. If he had been real, the detective Sergeant Cuff would undoubtedly have deduced that there was something a bit unusual about Collins' love life.

POLISH AUTHOR WROTE HIS POLISHED WORK IN ENGLISH

Joseph Conrad (born Jozef Teodor Konrad Korzeniowski) was Polish, but wrote his books in English despite not speaking that language fluently until he was an adult. Few authors were as successful writing in their non-native tongue.

Actually, English was Conrad's third language, having learned French as a youth.

"Youth" was one of Conrad's famous short stories, and his many novels included *Lord Jim* and *Heart of Darkness*—the latter inspiring Francis Ford Coppola's famous *Apocalypse Now* movie.

Like Herman Melville, Conrad (1857-1924) spent a lot of time at sea before becoming a published writer, and that experience later infused a number of his works—as did his move to England.

WHAT'S IN A NAME?
SOMETIMES SILLINESS

What's literature's silliest-sounding protagonist name? In the running is Natty Bumppo of *The Leatherstocking Tales*, the five **James Fenimore Cooper** novels that included *The Last of the Mohicans*.

But Bumppo is hardly silly himself. He's brave, loyal, self-sufficient, honest, quite a marksman with a rifle, and—for a white frontiersman of the 1700s—surprisingly nonracist when it comes to Native Americans.

Interestingly, Cooper (1789-1851) penned *The Leatherstocking Tales* out of chronological order; for instance, *The Deerslayer* was written last, yet it features Natty when he's youngest. That riveting novel combines cliff-hanging adventure with romantic tension that turns out to be one-sided.

Several other fascinating facts about Cooper? His father, William, established Cooperstown—the New York burg that later became famous for its Baseball Hall of Fame. James himself was kicked out of Yale for pranks, one of which reportedly involved tying a donkey to a professor's chair. Cooper was visited by Scotland's Sir Walter Scott in 1826 while the American author was living in Europe for several years. And Honoré de Balzac was among the European admirers of Cooper's work.

Getting back to memorable monikers, *The Deerslayer* also includes the characters Hurry Harry (a nickname) and Hetty Hutter.

HE COULD HAVE DONE NEWSPAPER REVIEWS OF HIS OWN WORK

Robertson Davies (1913-1995) of Canada mixed a long literary career with a long newspaper career.

During and after his time as a newspaper editor, publisher, and co-owner, Davies managed to also write eleven novels, fifteen plays, and other works. Sometimes, the two careers intersected.

For instance, Davies' novel *Murther & Walking Spirits* initially features three newspaper people: one who is murdered (Gil Gilmartin), one who's the killer, and one who's the wife of Gilmartin as well as the lover of the killer. The book then mostly veers into a chronicle of Gilmartin's ancestors as the "spirit" of the murdered man watches movies. But that's another (non-newspaper) story.

Davies, who also lived the university life teaching literature starting in the 1960s, was a close friend of John Irving. The American novelist put indirect references to Davies' novels in *A Prayer for Owen Meany* and spoke at Davies' funeral.

HE WAS NOT THE MAN
IN THE HIGH INCOME

A painful irony related to **Philip K. Dick** (1928-1982) is that he lived his life in near poverty yet several films based on his work did very well at the box office when released after he died.

Among them were *Blade Runner* (adapted from Dick's *Do Androids Dream of Electric Sheep?*) and *Total Recall* (based on his short story "We Can Remember It for You Wholesale"). And, more recently, his *The Man in the High Castle* alternative-history novel was turned into a TV drama.

Dick wrote 44 novels and 121 stories (the 165 works were mostly science-fiction) during his relatively short life. His health wasn't helped by drug use, and even winning some major sci-fi awards didn't lead to enough extra money to ease his financial stress.

Another sadly interesting fact about Dick is that the death of his twin sister Jane at the age of six weeks had such a major impact on his psyche that a recurring theme in his fiction is a phantom sibling. In *Dr. Bloodmoney*, for instance, a girl (Edie) conceived during a nuclear holocaust has a tiny brother (Bill) born inside her.

Also interesting: Dick simultaneously attended the same Berkeley, California high school as another future sci-fi legend: Ursula K. Le Guin. And sci-fi icon Robert A. Heinlein helped Dick financially at one point despite the two men having never met and Heinlein being more conservative in his politics and lifestyle than the ill-fated Dick.

AN INTERESTING *TWIST* IN AN AUTHOR'S LIFE

There were few blemishes in **Charles Dickens'** magnificent writing career, but one of them was what many labeled anti-Semitism in *Oliver Twist*.

Dickens (1812-1870) defended himself by arguing he was not prejudiced against Jews and that, in his 1838 novel, Jews were often in Fagin's class of criminals during the time the story was set. But Dickens apparently had second thoughts in 1860, when the wife of a man who had purchased the British author's home complained in a letter about how *Oliver Twist* "encouraged a vile prejudice against the despised Hebrew." Dickens responded by taking out many mentions of Fagin's Judaism in a printing of the novel.

Other facts about Dickens are well known: He was forced as a boy to leave school and work long days in a factory after his father was thrown into debtors' prison—stirring the future author's outrage against injustice. Serializing his novels, installment by installment, sometimes resulted in reader reaction influencing the content of future chapters—as when flagging sales caused Dickens to send the star of *Martin Chuzzlewit* to America. And the author wrote many iconic novels, including *A Christmas Carol*, *Bleak House*, *A Tale of Two Cities*, *Great Expectations*, etc. The also-famous *David Copperfield* was semi-autobiographical, as the reversed initials of Dickens' name indicate.

Then there were the author's two visits to the U.S. in 1842 and 1867-68. During the second trip's speaking tour, Mark Twain was an audience member.

Final fact: One of Dickens' young coworkers at the aforementioned factory was Bob Fagin—whose name would later be used in *Oliver Twist*.

HE MIXED HISTORY AND FICTION—AND THE NOVEL AND MEMOIR

E.L. Doctorow (1931-2015) is best known for novels such as *Ragtime*, but he also worked in an interesting genre one might call the "movel" or "nemoir."

The book he wrote that most fits this hybrid model was *World's Fair* (1985), which is basically a memoir in novel form starring a Bronx-born boy much like Doctorow and a family much like Doctorow's family. E.L. often wrote historical fiction, but *World's Fair* was *personal* historical fiction.

Edgar Lawrence Doctorow, whose parents deliberately gave him the same first name as Edgar Allan Poe, wrote his first two novels in the 1960s—while spending much of that decade as an NAL and Dial Press editor to make ends meet. He worked with notable authors such as James Baldwin, Ian Fleming, Norman Mailer, and Ayn Rand before eventually becoming as famous, or almost as famous, a writer as them.

Ragtime (1975) was the novel that sent Doctorow into the authorial stratosphere. In it, he mingled fictional characters with real historical figures like Henry Ford, Sigmund Freud, Emma Goldman, Harry Houdini, J.P. Morgan, and Booker T. Washington. *Ragtime* later became a movie and a Broadway musical.

Among Doctorow's other novels were *The Book of Daniel* (about the Rosenbergs in the McCarthy era) and *Billy Bathgate*—both of which also inspired films. Or maybe "nilms" or "fovels?"

A LATE AUTHOR EVEN WHEN ALIVE

L iterature lovers know about young phenoms—such as Mary Shelley (*Frankenstein*) and Carson McCullers (*The Heart Is a Lonely Hunter*)—who published exceptional debut novels when not much older than twenty.

Then there's the other extreme, exemplified by **Harriet Doerr** (1910-2002), whose first book came out when she was … seventy-four! That was *Stones for Ibarra* (1984), an exceptional novel with some autobiographical elements about an American couple trying to make a go of it in a remote region of Mexico.

The California-based Doerr—who wrote two other books published in her eighties—also admirably returned to college to complete her studies a half-century after starting. That made her a senior who was a senior.

WHAT SHAPED THE NOVELS TO COME

Fyodor **Dostoyevsky**'s superb novels address intensely consequential issues—crime and punishment (of course), economic inequality, utopianism, family, death, fate, fear, guilt, masochism, sadism, religion, repentance, redemption, and more. One reason for the Russian author's intense take on life was the fact that he came within an eyelash of losing his.

That was in St. Petersburg in 1849, when Dostoyevsky was sentenced to death for his (not very deep) involvement with a social-reform group. He was actually lined up for execution by firing squad, but the order was stayed at the last minute. Dostoyevsky (1821-1881) was instead sentenced to four years of exile and hard labor in Siberia—a time recounted in his 1862 novel/memoir *Notes from a Dead House*, which prefigured *Crime and Punishment*.

Crime and Punishment (1866) also reflected the health problems and grinding poverty Dostoyevsky experienced after his release from prison. And the amazing/pioneering psychological elements in that novel are said to have influenced Sigmund Freud, among others.

One of the high points of Dostoyevsky's life was getting a rapturous reception when speaking at the unveiling of a monument to famed Russian writer Alexander Pushkin in 1880, the same year Dostoyevsky completed *The Brothers Karamazov*. With its sprawling take on the Russian character and the human condition, that masterpiece strikes some readers as even better than *Crime and Punishment*. Dostoyevsky died just months after finishing *Karamazov*, which might have been the first of a trilogy.

IN THE MIDDLE OF A MARCH TOWARD MALE PROTAGONISTS

When it comes to the percentage of opposite-gender title characters, few renowned authors can top **George Eliot** (Mary Ann Evans). Four of the seven novels she wrote have male-named titles: *Adam Bede*, *Silas Marner*, *Daniel Deronda*, and *Felix Holt, the Radical*.

Eliot (1819-1880) obviously wanted to be taken seriously during an era in which intelligent women were often *not* taken seriously. Hence, a *nom de plume* as male as some of her book titles.

Of course, Eliot created strong female characters, too. For instance, Methodist preacher Dinah Morris of *Adam Bede* is a woman ahead of her time in that novel's late-eighteenth-century/early-nineteenth-century setting. There's also the brainy, imaginative, and sensitive Maggie Tulliver of the tragic, semi-autobiographical *The Mill on the Floss*. Eliot is clearly indignant that Maggie, as a female, has fewer opportunities for an education and freedom of action than her not-intellectual, stubborn brother Tom. And the gender of the smart and compassionate Dorothea Brooke often puts her at a societal disadvantage in the sprawling masterpiece *Middlemarch*.

Eliot also bucked Victorian Age convention in other ways—having an open, long-term relationship with the married George

Henry Lewes and then, after his death, wedding the two-decades-younger John Cross. Still, the traditional Queen Victoria was among the fans of Eliot's widely read novels, which made enough money in the author's lifetime to even satisfy Silas Marner during his miser period.

AN *AUGUST* WRITER

I t's uncanny how some authors have such a strong influence on later authors that you feel they almost share the same DNA. Such was the impact **William Faulkner** (1897-1962) had on Cormac McCarthy. The latter, highly original novelist is hardly an imitator of Faulkner, but there is often a similar Southern Gothic vibe between the two authors in the narration, prose, dialogue, characters (many downtrodden), and almost-biblical-like approach. Read something like McCarthy's *Outer Dark* or *Suttree*, and you will think of Faulkner novels such as *Light in August*.

Faulkner—whose writing would win him the Nobel Prize and two Pulitzers—spent much of his life in his native Mississippi. (There were also sojourns in places such as New Orleans, Virginia, and, as a screenwriter, in California.) His birth last name was actually Falkner.

The author's best-known novel could be *The Sound and the Fury* (1929), a highly experimental work that might have partly been inspired by Faulkner's annoyance with having a previous book rejected by a publisher. It was said the author figured, what the heck, he might as well write in a way he really wanted to write. *As I Lay Dying* (1930) continued in that fractured storytelling vein, but in an easier-to-follow way.

A number of Faulkner's other novels are more linear, but almost always deep—as writers such as Cormac McCarthy can attest.

A FAMILY TREE WITH PATRIOTIC AND UNPATRIOTIC ROOTS

F. **Scott Fitzgerald** (1896-1940) ended *The Great Gatsby* with perhaps the most famous last line in literature: "So we beat on, boats against the current, borne back ceaselessly into the past."

Fitzgerald's own past included two memorable ancestors.

One was Francis Scott Key (1779-1843), who penned the words to "The Star-Spangled Banner." That cousin several times removed would become the namesake of the twentieth-century author, whose full name was Francis Scott Key Fitzgerald.

The other distant relative was Mary Surratt, who was executed in 1865 for taking part in the conspiracy to assassinate Abraham Lincoln.

Fitzgerald also wrote novels such as *Tender Is the Night* (considered a partly autobiographical take on his life with mentally ill wife Zelda) and *This Side of Paradise*.

If paradise exists, Francis Scott Key and Mary Surratt might be on different sides of it—as in one being in and the other not.

A FATEFUL MISSED PROCEDURE

L iterary prizes are almost always welcome, but an award won by New Zealand writer **Janet Frame** literally saved her career.

Frame (1924-2004) was scheduled for a lobotomy after years of serious psychiatric issues. But the procedure was canceled when her debut collection of short stories unexpectedly won a prestigious national prize.

There would only be two more short-story collections in Frame's career, but thirteen novels—including perhaps her best-known one: the intriguingly titled *Yellow Flowers in the Antipodean Room*. She also wrote children's fiction, poetry, essays, and three autobiographies that inspired the film *An Angel at My Table* directed by Jane Campion of *The Piano* fame.

Frame's father worked for New Zealand's railways and her mother was a housemaid to the family of renowned writer Katherine Mansfield. Two of Janet's sisters drowned and her brother had epilepsy—all of which undoubtedly influenced her fiction.

The author, who spent a number of years in Europe and the U.S., won about two-dozen other major New Zealand awards in addition to the one that saved her career.

LIFE OF THE WRITER WHO WROTE *THE LIFE OF CHARLOTTE BRONTË*

Elizabeth Gaskell (1810-1865) is best known for writing *The Life of Charlotte Brontë*—the first biography of the famous *Jane Eyre* author. But Mrs. Gaskell (as the mother of five is often referred to) was a novelist in her own right.

Among her most-remembered works is *Cranford*, which originated as a series of 1851-53 stories in the *Household Words* magazine edited by Charles Dickens. The tales—which were turned into a loosely connected novel—focus on the "spinster" women of a small English town, class differences there, and more. Penned with a funny, light touch, *Cranford* is also poignant—and a valuable time capsule of life in a village just starting to be touched by modernity and some non-English influences. Plus the book includes a brief, tragicomic subplot involving Dickens' novel *The Posthumous Papers of the Pickwick Club*.

Gaskell was friends with Charlotte Brontë—and it was Brontë's father, Patrick, who asked to have the biography of Charlotte written several months after she died in 1855.

Another connection to a *very* famous writer: a memorial panel to Gaskell in Poets' Corner of Westminster Abbey is in a window above the tomb of *The Canterbury Tales* author Geoffrey Chaucer.

"THE YELLOW WALLPAPER" FEATURED A WOMAN WHO FELT BLUE

In the very patriarchal time of the nineteenth century, some female authors tried to break their female characters out of gender restrictions. Among those making the effort were Mary Shelley, Anne Brontë, George Eliot, Kate Chopin, and **Charlotte Perkins Gilman** (1860-1935).

The last of those five names is not familiar to many people today, but in her time Gilman was a prominent feminist, intellectual, lecturer, teacher, painter, magazine editor, nonfiction writer, and fiction writer perhaps best known for her short story "The Yellow Wallpaper." That riveting tale focuses on a wife who wants to work and have mental stimulation, but her patronizing physician husband, others, and society in general treat her almost like an invalid child. As she impotently tries to fight this monotony and oppression, the results are chilling. Not surprisingly, Gilman had difficulty getting the story published—it was written in 1890, but didn't appear in print until 1892.

Gilman's best-known nonfiction book might be *Women and Economics* (1898), a hard-hitting work used in college courses and translated into seven languages.

Born in Connecticut, Gilman was a resident of California at the time of her death; she committed suicide while suffering from terminal cancer.

Gilman's great-aunt was another writer who broke the mold: Harriet Beecher Stowe of *Uncle Tom's Cabin* fame.

THE VISITS TO OLD GOETHE

What if you're the author of numerous works, yet a novella you penned as a very young man is the only one most visitors want to talk about in your senior years?

That was the case with **Johann Wolfgang von Goethe** (1749-1832), who immediately became ultra-famous after writing *The Sorrows of Young Werther* at age twenty-four. According to poet W.H. Auden's foreword in a 1971 edition of *Werther*, many people who made the pilgrimage to see the elderly Goethe in Weimar, Germany, had read nothing else by the author but his youthful novella.

Goethe was somewhat annoyed by this, but there's no denying the appeal of the heartfelt, seemingly simple, yet very wise tale of the sensitive, depressed, romantically obsessed Werther character.

Examples of other renowned Goethe works those visitors weren't as familiar with? Try the drama *Faust*, to name one. The second part of *Faust* was completed near the end of Goethe's life, presumably when those one-track-mind visitors weren't there to take up the author's writing time.

The theme of one's soul being sold to the devil has surfaced in all kinds of fiction, including Douglass Wallop's novel *The Year the Yankees Lost the Pennant* (which inspired the hit Broadway musical *Damn Yankees*). The protagonist of Wallop's book was a fan of baseball's Washington Senators, which reminds me that Goethe worked in government in addition to writing.

THE INFLUENCE OF AN OVERCOAT CAN'T BE OVERSTATED

For an author who wrote a novel titled *Dead Souls*, the work of **Nikolai Gogol** (1809-1852) remained very much alive after his premature passing.

Gogol's depressing/mesmerizing short story "The Overcoat" influenced later Russian literature so much that Fyodor Dostoyevsky reportedly said "we have all come out from under Gogol's 'Overcoat'"—and also mentioned Gogol in *Crime and Punishment*. Then, nearly two centuries after Nikolai's birth, the Indian-American son in Jhumpa Lahiri's 2004 novel *The Namesake* was given the nickname Gogol because his father survived a horrific train crash while clutching a collection of the Ukrainian-born author's tales.

The often-satirical Gogol is considered an early master of the short story along with writers such as Nathaniel Hawthorne, Edgar Allan Poe, and Alexander Pushkin. Like Hawthorne, Gogol spent a significant amount of time living in Italy—and also traveled in Germany and Switzerland, spent the winter of 1836-37 in Paris, and took a pilgrimage to Jerusalem about a decade later.

Gogol was buried in the Danilov Monastery in Moscow. When the monastery was demolished in 1931 and the author's remains exhumed for transfer to a cemetery, his body was discovered to be lying face down—leading to theories that Gogol may have been buried alive. That was as spooky as Akaky in "The Overcoat" returning as a ghost to take overcoats from people after his beloved, hard-earned overcoat had been stolen when he was alive.

A PROSE MASTER OF THE POLITICAL AND THE PERSONAL

South African author **Nadine Gordimer** (1923-2014) wrote about the onerous effects of apartheid in many of her novels, and was also an activist in the anti-apartheid movement. One example of that activism was helping to edit the famous 1964 "I Am Prepared to Die" courtroom speech Nelson Mandela made before he was sentenced to a long prison term.

The white Gordimer also spoke against apartheid, attended demonstrations, hid African National Congress members in her home, and more. Meanwhile, she had several of her works—including *July's People*—banned by the apartheid government.

But Gordimer's novels were more nuanced and complex than polemic. For instance, 1990's *My Son's Story*—which helped its author win the Nobel Prize in Literature the following year—has a mixed-race protagonist (Sonny) who is both admirable for his risky political work and not admirable as a married man having an affair (with a white activist).

Interestingly, Gordimer and her close friend Mandela (1918-2013) died less than eight months apart.

LONG MARRIAGE AND AN EVEN LONGER LIST OF BOOKS

Which famous author had the longest marriage? One strong candidate is **Graham Greene** (1904-1991), who was wed to his wife Vivien for a whopping sixty-four years (1927 until his death).

But it was a marriage in name only for the vast majority of those years. Greene had two other lengthy relationships and various affairs, but Vivien wouldn't divorce him because of her Catholicism.

Of course, Greene is better known for his writing output than his personal life. The popular British author penned novels (including *The Power and the Glory*, *The End of the Affair*, and *The Quiet American*), autobiographies, travel books, plays, screenplays (such as *The Third Man*), children's books, essays, and short stories. One of those stories—the six-page, mind-blowing "Proof Positive"—would have done Edgar Allan Poe proud.

Speaking of other writers, Greene's mother was a cousin to Robert Louis Stevenson. And speaking of other notable men, Charlie Chaplin and Greene were close friends while both spent their later years in Switzerland.

Herman Wouk (*The Caine Mutiny*, *Marjorie Morningstar*, and *The Winds of War*) may be one of the few famous authors to surpass Greene in marriage longevity; Wouk and his wife Betty were wed for sixty-six years until her death in 2011.

HE EXCELLED IN IMAGINATION AND AMALGAMATION

Two books, fiction and nonfiction, that are among the most famous of the twentieth century were written by one author.

Those would be *Roots* and *The Autobiography of Malcolm X*, both by **Alex Haley** (1921-1992). To be more specific, the latter book was ghostwritten—based on dozens of interviews Haley conducted with the African-American leader.

But was *Roots* (1976) totally a novel? No, it was a partly fictionalized account of Haley's family tree. And some passages may have been plagiarized, with the author settling a lawsuit to that effect.

Still, Haley spent more than a decade researching the riveting *Roots*, which became a massive bestseller, inspired the 1977 miniseries that drew a record-breaking audience of 130 million, and sparked general interest in genealogy.

Before *The Autobiography of Malcolm X* was published in 1965 (the year its subject was assassinated), Haley conducted many high-profile interviews for *Playboy* magazine with such people as the Reverend Dr. Martin Luther King, Jr., boxer Muhammad Ali, music producer Quincy Jones, football's Jim Brown, TV host Johnny Carson, and vile American Nazi Party leader George Lincoln Rockwell.

Haley was such a skillful writer that, during his long 1939-1959 Coast Guard career, many fellow sailors paid him to pen love letters to their girlfriends.

THE TWO-PART LIFE OF ONE WRITER

Thomas Hardy (1840-1928) was best known as a novelist during the first half of his career and as a poet during the second half. Indeed, his last novel (*Uude the Obscure*) came out in 1895, and all his poetry collections were published from the 1890s on.

Amid his most famous fictional works (*Far from the Madding Crowd*, *The Return of the Native*, *The Mayor of Casterbridge*, and *Tess of the d'Urbervilles*), Hardy wrote a less-known novel called *The Hand of Ethelberta*. That 1876 book's resourceful title character is a poet, among other things—perhaps an early indication of Hardy's regard for the versifying profession?

There's also something poetic and novel about where Hardy's remains ended up in England. His heart is buried at a Hardy family site in Dorset, while his ashes are interred in the famous Poets' Corner of London's Westminster Abbey. Yes, poetic and novel, but the Hardy family was upset that the author's body was separated and that all of it didn't end up in Dorset. There was even gruesome talk about a cat eating Hardy's heart just after it was extracted.

Hardy's second wife (his secretary) was nearly forty years younger than him. That May-December union was also sort of presaged in *The Hand of Ethelberta*, whose title character agrees to marry a rich, much older man in order to provide for her struggling family. The novel has been interpreted as a way for Hardy to address class differences—a theme he poetically excelled at in various novels.

RAPPACCINI'S PRESIDENTIAL CANDIDATE

Which famous novelist used political spin to land in Liverpool before the Beatles? **Nathaniel Hawthorne** (1804-1864), who wrote a puffy campaign biography of his pal Franklin Pierce and was rewarded for that 1852 book with the job of U.S. consul in Liverpool after the lackluster Pierce became president. Pierce and Hawthorne had been classmates at Maine's Bowdoin College (along with Henry Wadsworth Longfellow).

After his consul stint, Hawthorne took advantage of his proximity to Europe's mainland to spend time in Italy—a sojourn that provided material for his last completed novel, *The Marble Faun*.

Hawthorne, of course, was also known for other novels such as *The House of the Seven Gables* and for his many short stories—including "Rappaccini's Daughter."

The author may have made important contacts at college, but there's no truth to the rumor that Hester Prynne of Hawthorne's masterpiece *The Scarlet Letter* said in high school: "I was given an 'A,' but are my SAT scores high enough?"

To Whom a Prize Didn't Go

Ernest Hemingway (1899-1961) won a Pulitzer Prize for *The Old Man and the Sea* in 1953, but a Pulitzer for a much better book—*For Whom the Bell Tolls*—was yanked from him a dozen years earlier.

A Pulitzer committee and the Pulitzer board recommended the prize for Hemingway's riveting novel of the Spanish Civil War, but Columbia University President Nicholas Murray Butler overrode both—resulting in no prize being awarded that year to any novel.

Apparently, Butler found the book offensive. For its candid language? For its sex scenes? For its anti-fascism? (The longtime Columbia president was sympathetic to Mussolini and Hitler for a while.) Whatever the reason, "the Butler did it" ... stupidly.

Hemingway's prose style in *For Whom the Bell Tolls* and most of his other fiction was terse and understated—and, partly for those two reasons, a huge influence on a number of modern authors. His writing approach partly stemmed from his early journalistic experiences, including a short stint at *The Kansas City Star*. Various other famous novelists—including Mark Twain and Gabriel Garcia Marquez—were also journalists in their younger years.

Butler couldn't prevent Hemingway from winning the 1954 Nobel Prize in Literature, because the university president died in 1947.

Ironically, Columbia's library is named after Butler.

YOU'VE GOT JAIL, AND SUBSEQUENT FAME

There were several surprising things about **O. Henry** (1862-1910) in addition to the surprise endings to many of his short stories.

For instance, did you know he coined the term "banana republic" while on the lam in Central America?

And did you know that O. Henry was on the lam? He was accused of embezzling from a Texas bank he had worked for and fled the U.S. to avoid a trial. The North Carolina native later returned to be with his dying wife, and was jailed in Ohio from 1898 to 1901. He wrote some short stories while in prison, using various aliases such as … O. Henry. (His real name was William Sydney Porter.)

Soon after his release, Porter began writing many more stories—including beloved classics with clever twists such as "The Gift of the Magi," "The Ransom of Red Chief," "The Cop and the Anthem," and "The Last Leaf."

After O. Henry died, there were efforts to get him a presidential pardon—not because he was innocent of embezzling, but because his behavior was exemplary during and after prison. Those efforts were as unsuccessful as Porter was successful (in attracting readers).

THE HALLUCINATORY HERMANN HESSE

When one hears Steppenwolf sing "Born to Be Wild" and "Magic Carpet Ride," one realizes just how appropriate that rock band's name is. After all, **Hermann Hesse**'s striking novel *Steppenwolf* features a character (Harry Haller) who supposedly has a wild wolf side, and the book's hallucinatory conclusion takes place at a "Magic Theatre."

Also, let's not forget San Francisco's Magic Theatre and Chicago's Steppenwolf Theatre.

Speaking of names, it's not a coincidence that Harry Haller shared Hermann Hesse's initials, and that the Hermine character's moniker in *Steppenwolf* is a female variation of Hermann.

During his lifetime, Hesse (1877-1962) was a widely read author in Europe but not so much in the United States. Soon after his death, however, many members of the U.S. counterculture became enamored with his work and sales skyrocketed not only in America but back in Europe as well. Another prominent band, Santana, even named its 1970 album "Abraxas" after a word in Hesse's novel *Demian*.

The German-Swiss author, who was influenced by Indian culture and Buddhist philosophy, is also well remembered for his novel *Siddhartha*.

Hesse won the Nobel Prize in Literature in 1946—two years after the birth of Steppenwolf's John Kay and one year before the birth of Carlos Santana.

NO STRANGER TO THE SUCCESS TRAIN

How's this for early writing success? **Patricia Highsmith** (1921-1995) saw her *Strangers on a Train* novel published in 1950 (when she was twenty-nine) and the movie version of that book brought to the big screen by Alfred Hitchcock in 1951 (when Highsmith was thirty).

But as happy as readers and filmgoers were with her psychological thrillers, Highsmith did not live a happy life. She endured depression, various physical ailments, and alcoholism—and was gay at a time when that was far from easy. Perhaps because of all those difficulties, Highsmith was said to have had a mean streak—but not with the animals she loved.

Highsmith authored a total of twenty-two novels, including others that also inspired movies. Five of those books—*The Talented Mr. Ripley* is one—starred the rather amoral Tom Ripley and depicted his skirting-the-law shenanigans. In *Ripley's Game*, for instance, Tom sets up a situation where someone who casually snubbed him is lured into murdering some mafioso for money—and things don't end well.

The Texas-born Highsmith (real name: Mary Patricia Plangman) also wrote for comic books for a while! But her intense novels, while not without humor, were far from comic.

WOMEN OF LETTERS: "A" HELPED US REMEMBER "Z"

The first name of *Their Eyes Were Watching God* author **Zora Neale Hurston** (1891-1960) may be alphabetically last on many lists of great authors, but there were firsts and near-firsts in her life.

Hurston spent part of her childhood in Eatonville, Florida—America's first all-black incorporated township. She was also one of the first African-American students to attend the New York City-based Barnard College, where Zora majored in anthropology and worked in that field of study with fellow Barnard alum Margaret Mead.

Perhaps the most renowned black woman writer of the twentieth century's first half, Hurston was practically forgotten after her death. Interest revived mostly because of a writer with an early-in-the-alphabet first name: Alice Walker.

The future author of *The Color Purple* found what she believed to be Hurston's unmarked Florida grave in 1973 and wrote an influential *Ms.* magazine article about Zora two years later. Then Walker's eyes watched Hurston's name deservedly reenter the public consciousness.

SOMETIMES A DOOR IS MORE THAN A DOOR

Aldous Huxley (1894-1963) is of course best known for penning the dystopian classic *Brave New World*, but he also has a lesser-known claim to fame: His 1954 book *The Doors of Perception* inspired the name of The Doors rock group—whose lead singer/lyricist, Jim Morrison, had a literary bent.

But there's another link in that chain. The title of Huxley's book came from a line in William Blake's 1793 work *The Marriage of Heaven and Hell*.

Huxley was a British writer of novels, essays, and more who eventually settled in Southern California—where The Doors were formed two years after his death. Aldous was among the famous authors who took a stab at Hollywood screenplays, working on movies such as those based on the classics *Pride and Prejudice* and *Jane Eyre*. Some of Huxley's own fiction, including *Point Counter Point*, was in the classic rather than dystopian mold.

Speaking of dystopian events, John F. Kennedy's November 22, 1963 assassination happened on the same day Huxley (and writer C.S. Lewis) died. JFK was also known as an author; his *Profiles in Courage* won a Pulitzer Prize, but much of that book may have been ghostwritten by Theodore Sorensen. If the Pulitzer judges made their *Profiles* decision in a room with more than one entrance, they didn't display much perception after walking through the doors.

HAUNTING WORK EVEN WHEN *HAUNTING* WASN'T IN THE TITLE

S hirley Jackson is not as famous as many of her mid-twenti-eth-century author peers—perhaps because being a woman got her dismissed by some readers and critics. But many people are aware of her two best-known titles: the spooky 1948 tale "The Lottery" (seen in many a short-story anthology) and the also-spooky 1959 novel *The Haunting of Hill House* (which inspired the 1963 movie *The Haunting*).

Those two literary works feature subtle, slow-building horror that really sticks with readers—and has also stuck with Jackson-in-fluenced writers such as Stephen King and Richard Matheson. But some readers were furious when "The Lottery" was first published (in *The New Yorker* magazine) because "bucolic" small-town life was shown to have quite a disturbing underbelly. And, by extension, civilization in general was depicted as not always ... civilized.

Jackson (1916-1965) also penned sardonic, humorous works that had somewhat the feel of later writing by Erma Bombeck. Those works were inspired by Jackson's family; the lottery of life gave Shirley and her husband, noted literary critic Stanley Edgar Hyman, four children.

THE AMERICAN WHO BECAME AN ENGLISHMAN

A uthors often pick their characters' names for specific reasons. For instance, **Henry James** (1843-1916) gave the protagonist in his 1877 novel *The American* the very American name of Christopher Newman to evoke Christopher Columbus and a "New Man" from the "New World" rather than Europe—where Newman moved after making his fortune in the U.S.

Indeed, James' psychologically intimate writing often focused on the interactions of Americans and Europeans, and the clash of those two cultures. *The Ambassadors* is certainly another example of that.

James himself was American-born (in New York City, the setting of some of his novels, such as *Washington Square*) and lived many decades in Europe. He even became a British citizen the year before his death, apparently to protest the initial reluctance of the U.S. government to enter World War I.

James wrote more than twenty novels—many of them classics, such as *The Portrait of a Lady*—as well as numerous novellas, short stories, plays, and nonfiction works. His later work became more complex, with prose that some readers and critics admired greatly and others found a bit of a slog to get through.

The author's personal life was complex as well; he never married, and perhaps was gay, while also maintaining deep friendships with various women.

That aforementioned Newman name might have inspired James' close pal Edith Wharton to give the male protagonist in her 1920 novel *The Age of Innocence* the first name of Newland.

A LATE START AND AN IMPRESSIVE FINISH

There are many distinctive things connected with the life and career of English mystery writer **P.D. James** (1920-2014).

Phyllis Dorothy's first novel wasn't published until 1962 (when she was forty-two) and her last novel came out in 2011 (when the author was an impressive ninety-plus). She managed to write more than twenty books (including some nonfiction) despite her late start, despite dealing with a mentally ill husband, and despite spending many years holding non-author jobs—including government positions in forensic science and criminal science that were, of course, not unrelated to her writing.

Also, James' novels blurred the line between crime fiction and literary fiction. So it's no surprise that her most famous character—Adam Dalgliesh—was a detective *and* a poet. And James' last novel, *Death Comes to Pemberley*, is a sequel of sorts to Jane Austen's *Pride and Prejudice*.

While James' main genre was crime/mystery, she also wrote the dystopian novel *The Children of Men*, which became a movie. Many of her other novels were also turned into film or TV productions. Heck, after being caught, the double killer in James' *The Lighthouse* was looking forward to his case being on screens of the news-program sort. And that murderer had some legitimate reasons for being angry with his first victim—a novelist!

WHEN IRISH AUTHORS AREN'T SMILING

History is replete with clueless and/or timid publishers rejecting books that later became classics. Such was the case with **James Joyce**'s *Dubliners* short-story collection, which includes the iconic tale "The Dead."

Joyce (1882-1941) first tried to get the collection published in 1905. Over the ensuing years, there were twists and turns—with more than one near-agreement, more than one publisher wanting significant cuts or changes, etc.

Why? Possible reasons include the stories' subtlety, psychological complexity, and scarcity of traditional plot—as well as the use of some frank language that would seem tame today.

After rejections from fifteen publishers, *Dubliners* finally came out in 1914. The publisher? Grant Richards Ltd., which had rejected the manuscript nine years earlier. The company used page proofs Joyce managed to save after another printer burned the other copies.

Joyce, of course, went on to write additional classics such as *A Portrait of the Artist as a Young Man* and *Ulysses*.

SOMETIMES THE BEST BOOK ISN'T THE MOST FAMOUS BOOK

Ken Kesey (1935-2001) is known most for his 1962 debut novel *One Flew Over the Cuckoo's Nest*, which was turned into a multi-Oscar-winning film thirteen years later. He's perhaps known secondly for being a counterculture figure during the 1960s. But *Sometimes a Great Notion*—the 1964 novel Kesey wrote after *One Flew*—remains woefully underrated.

Sometimes is a *tour de force*—a long, sprawling look at an Oregon lumber town, two feuding half-brothers who come together again as adults, a bitter labor strike, rotten weather, and the meaning (or lack of meaning) of life. The way Kesey frequently changes the narrative perspective from character to character (and there are many of them) is among the impressive aspects of the novel.

In an introduction to one *Sometimes* edition, author Charles Bowden called it "one of the few essential books written by an American in the last half century."

The Colorado-born Kesey grew up in Oregon and graduated from the University of Oregon. Later, a group called the Merry Pranksters grew around Kesey—and their cross-country trip in a school bus, their parties, and their LSD use were chronicled in Tom Wolfe's *The Electric Kool-Aid Acid Test*. Pranksters members included bohemian figures, writers, and the band that would become the Grateful Dead. But after being arrested and jailed for drug possession, a fake suicide, and escaping to Mexico, Kesey lived a more sedate lifestyle focused on writing, teaching, and family. Not a bad notion.

A Book Leaps Like a Big Cat into Literary History

Giuseppe Tomasi di Lampedusa (1896-1957) wrote only one novel, and it didn't appear until the year after he died from lung cancer. But what a book *The Leopard* was: richly written, evocative, melancholy, earthy, and more.

The Sicily-set historical novel stars a prince ("The Leopard" of the title) living in a nineteenth-century Italy transitioning from a declining aristocracy to something resembling a democracy. Lampedusa finished the book in 1956, but—in yet another case of literary merit not being quickly recognized—it was turned down by two publishers. Later, it would become the best-selling novel in Italian history.

Some people in Italy's book business were aware of *The Leopard*'s merit, but the novel was perceived as potentially controversial. Indeed, after it was released, it was criticized on the right for showing the nobility and clergy as rather decadent, and criticized on the left for depicting the nobility in too positive a light and for *not* depicting Italy's nineteenth-century unification and working class in a more enthusiastic way.

Lampedusa, who was of noble birth himself and used some family history for *The Leopard*, had the novel in mind from the time he was a young man. His original plan was to have the book take place in just a day (a la James Joyce's *Ulysses*), but he dropped that plan. The novel instead spans 1860 to 1910, though much of the action takes place between 1860 and 1862.

Despite its title, one of *The Leopard*'s most memorable characters is a dog that lived in the 1860s and is the focus of the book's last lines in 1910.

THE AUTHOR WHO KICKED UP TREMENDOUS SALES

G iven all the computer and digital elements in the three riveting *Millennium* novels by **Stieg Larsson** (1954-2004), it's appropriate that the Swedish writer posthumously became the first author to sell a million electronic copies of his work on Amazon's Kindle.

That trio of books, of course, includes *The Girl With the Dragon Tattoo*, *The Girl Who Played With Fire*, and *The Girl Who Kicked the Hornet's Nest*.

Those crime thrillers don't just take on small-potato malfeasance. They depict a huge swath of corrupt behavior in government, the upper reaches of law enforcement, the upper reaches of corporations, and more. But most of all they address violence against women in general and Lisbeth Salander in particular.

Lisbeth—one of the most original characters in recent literature—is a grievously wronged woman in her twenties whose experiences have made her angry and antisocial. She also has a photographic memory, brilliant computer-hacking skills, courage, and resourcefulness.

The other star of the novels is the charismatic Mikael Blomkvist, a forty-something investigative journalist who Larsson partly modeled on himself. One of Larsson's formative experiences, at age fifteen, was witnessing three friends rape a young girl. The future author was so outraged, and felt so guilty about not helping the girl, that he became a lifelong fighter against violence toward women—which any reader of his novels can see. And that's a lot of readers; the books have sold more than seventy-five million copies in all.

SONS AND LOVERS AND HERMAN MELVILLE

A number of lists have *Sons and Lovers* as one of the top ten novels of the twentieth century. Unfortunately, another "ten" that **D.H. Lawrence**'s 1913 book is known for is 10 percent of it being cut by its original publisher.

That happened because the novel contained some sexually explicit (for its time) passages and some strong (for its time) marital-strife scenes. Also, the publisher thought the semi-autobiographical book was too long. Lawrence reluctantly agreed to the butchering because he desperately needed the money from potential book sales—which were sadly poor during his lifetime but excellent (several million) in the years after his death.

There's more to *Sons and Lovers* than controversy. The novel portrays a mother too emotionally close to the sons of the title, looks at working-class life (the father in the novel, like Lawrence's dad, is a miner), etc.

David Herbert Richards Lawrence (1885-1930) also authored *Women in Love* and *Lady Chatterley's Lover*, among other books. (A whole lotta "love" in his novel titles ...) And he wrote poems, plays, essays, and literary criticism; painted; and, in his early years, taught.

Later in life, the Englishman lived in the United States and elsewhere. Harassment by British authorities over his antiwar views (during World War I) was a big reason for leaving his home country.

Lawrence—friends with Aldous Huxley, another Englishman who moved to the U.S.—also wrote the *Studies in Classic American Literature* book that helped posthumously revive the reputation of Herman Melville.

MEMORABLE CHARACTERS HAD MEMORABLE NAMES

The novel with the most interesting character names? One candidate is *Where the Heart Is* by **Billie Letts** (1938-2014). Its protagonist is a young woman named Novalee Nation, and the book also features Americus Nation (her daughter) and friends such as Lexie Coop, Sister Husband, Forney Hull, Benny Goodluck, and Moses Whitecotton.

The heartwarming and compelling 1995 novel starts off with a pregnant teen (Novalee) abandoned by her nasty boyfriend in an Oklahoma Walmart during a trip from Tennessee to California. Then Novalee builds a life with the help of the above-named people.

Another interesting thing about *Where the Heart Is*—a bestseller after it became an Oprah's Book Club selection in 1998—is that it was a debut novel published when Letts was already in her mid-fifties. The author spent much of her career teaching creative writing at the college level.

Where the Heart Is became a 2000 movie that included Billie's husband Dennis Letts in a small role. (Their son is actor/playwright Tracy Letts, who penned *August: Osage County*.) The film starred actresses and actors with less colorful names than the roles they played: Natalie Portman (Novalee), Ashley Judd (Lexie), Keith David (Moses), etc. But Stockard Channing gave her Sister Husband character a run for the offbeat-name money.

THE SWEDISH ACADEMY LOVED THIS AMERICAN WRITER

After a run of memorable novels about the American experience, **Sinclair Lewis** (1885-1951) became the first American to win the Nobel Prize in Literature.

His Nobel year was 1930, and his run of 1920s novels included *Main Street, Babbitt, Arrowsmith, Elmer Gantry*, and *Dodsworth*.

Main Street, Lewis' seventh novel after six little-remembered books, was an instant success—selling 180,000 copies in its first six months and two million within several years.

The Minnesota-born Lewis—who sold story plots to Jack London during his younger years—often set his novels in the small towns of America's Midwest heartland and could be quite cutting in addressing capitalism, materialism, conformity, hypocrisy, religion, and so on. Lewis was also skilled at three-dimensionally depicting his characters, including strong female ones. Lewis' second wife, newspaper columnist Dorothy Thompson, was a formidable woman herself.

Lewis, also a prolific short-story writer, authored eleven novels after winning the Nobel. The best known was *It Can't Happen Here*, a dystopian tale of a fascist elected U.S. president. (Shades of 2016?) Also of note was 1947's *Kingsblood Royal*, which was unusual for its time in being a novel written by a white author that prominently featured and sympathetically portrayed a partly African-American character. *Ebony* magazine praised the novel highly.

EVERY DOG MUST HAVE HIS NOVEL

When one thinks of mirrors in fiction, Lewis Carroll's *Alice's Adventures in Wonderland* and *Through the Looking-Glass* come to mind. But **Jack London** (1876-1916) pulled off one of the great reflective feats in literary history with *The Call of the Wild* and *White Fang*—because those works are basically mirror images of each other.

The Call of the Wild (1903) is about a domesticated dog dragged from civilization in sunny California to a much more primitive existence in bitterly cold Alaska. *White Fang* (1906) focuses on a wild Alaskan wolf who eventually ends up living the good life with a family in California—though the animal has a couple of violent encounters in the Golden State (none involving hot tubs).

London's two books do share the non-mirrored similarity of being tense, absorbing, page-turning reads. And if they ever visited the two Lewis Carroll books, the alpha quadrupeds in *The Call of the Wild* and *White Fang* would have the characters in Alice's world nervously gulping beverages much stronger than tea.

AT THE MOUNTAINS OF POSTHUMOUS FAME

When it comes to minimal fame while living and maximum fame after dying, few authors can match **H.P. Lovecraft** (1890-1937).

Lovecraft's hypnotic horror fiction appeared mostly in pulp magazines during his relatively short life, and the sensitive/neurotic/uncomfortable-with-self-promotion writer was often impoverished to the point where he even went hungry on occasion. But his renown skyrocketed after his death; in fact, one of the many Facebook pages devoted to him had nearly a million likes as of 2016. And Lovecraft, who was influenced by writers such as Edgar Allan Poe, would influence later writers such as Stephen King, Clive Barker, and Neil Gaiman.

The Rhode Island-born Lovecraft mostly penned short stories ("The Colour Out of Space" and "The Shadow Out of Time" are among his best) but also wrote several novellas (including the eye-popping Antarctica adventure *At the Mountains of Madness*).

Though he didn't enjoy much success while living, the discouraged Lovecraft offered encouragement to aspiring writers in some of the thousands of letters he wrote.

A NATURAL WRITER WHO DIDN'T WRITE *THE NATURAL* MOVIE

Bernard Malamud (1914-1986) lived long enough to see his 1952 novel *The Natural* made into a 1984 movie of the same name starring Robert Redford. But the film wasn't an all-welcome development for Malamud and a number of critics because it changed his downbeat baseball book quite a bit and gave it a happy ending that didn't fit.

Gee, what a surprise for a Hollywood production.

The Brooklyn, New York-born Malamud was also known for compelling novels such as *The Assistant* and the Pulitzer Prize-winning *The Fixer*, as well as for his short stories. That all placed him—along with writers such as Saul Bellow, Philip Roth, and Isaac Bashevis Singer—as one of the twentieth century's most famous Jewish authors. And Jewish themes were often part of Malamud's work, though he was an agnostic who married a Catholic woman, Ann de Chiara.

Malamud became interested in literature early, and wrote a thesis on Thomas Hardy for the master's degree he earned at Columbia University. He later taught at Oregon State University and Vermont's Bennington College throughout much of his authorial career. Not surprisingly, his specialty at the latter institution was creative writing—which is rather different from the creative license taken by makers of *The Natural* movie.

CHRONICLE OF A SUCCESS NOT FORETOLD

Eighteen months of near solitude is what it took for **Gabriel Garcia Marquez** (1927-2014) to write *One Hundred Years of Solitude.*

Garcia Marquez was mostly known as a journalist when he began the magic-realism-infused novel in 1965. As he wrote, his wife Mercedes ran the not-rich household—and was forced to run up $12,000 in debt.

But the Colombian writer's financial gamble and creative inspiration paid off big time, as *One Hundred Years of Solitude* immediately became a runaway bestseller when published in 1967 and eventually sold millions of copies. It's also on many lists of the greatest novels of all time.

Why was the book so well received? *The New York Times* obituary of Garcia Marquez said: "In following the rise and fall of the Buendia family through several generations of war and peace, affluence and poverty, the novel seemed to many critics and readers the defining saga of Latin America's social and political history."

Garcia Marquez went on to write other memorable novels, including *Chronicle of a Death Foretold* and *Love in the Time of Cholera.* The latter is mostly about a briefly on/fifty years off/then on-again relationship, but that book also masterfully depicts romantic ardor of virtually every kind. *Love in the Time of Cholera* contains less magic realism than *One Hundred Years of Solitude*, but it's magical nonetheless—especially during the boat trip that ends the novel.

The Long and Short of an Author's Long Life

Many famous novelists lived short or relatively short lives: Jane Austen, the Brontë sisters, F. Scott Fitzgerald—the list goes on and on. But there were exceptions, of course, such as **W. Somerset Maugham** (1874-1965).

Before dying at the age of ninety-one, the British writer penned a huge number of novels, short stories, plays, travel books, and other works. Perhaps best known for his semi-autobiographical masterpiece *Of Human Bondage*, Maugham's top fiction also included *The Razor's Edge*, *The Moon and Sixpence*, *The Painted Veil*, and the less-famous *Cakes and Ale*—one of whose characters was novelist Edward Driffield, possibly based on Thomas Hardy.

In the introduction to a 1950 edition of the 1930-published *Cakes and Ale*, Maugham acknowledged some similarities between Driffield and Hardy, but pointed out many differences and noted that he had met Hardy only once. Maugham also wrote in the intro that *Cakes and Ale* was his favorite book because it contained his "most engaging heroine": Driffield's first wife Rosie, based on a woman Maugham once knew.

Maugham was gay, though he married at one point. Other interesting facts: The author was a spy during World War I, and his *Ashenden: Or the British Agent* stories were said to have influenced Ian Fleming's creation of James Bond. Also, Maugham trained as a doctor before becoming an author, and later said the time was not wasted because he got a chance to learn about all kinds of people and emotions. Who knows, maybe that medical background also gave Maugham a few habits that helped him live a long life.

HE WROTE MANY JEWELS BESIDES "THE NECKLACE"

Some writers are known mostly for one novel or short story. But that doesn't mean they didn't pen other excellent works.

Such is the case with **Guy de Maupassant** (1850-1893). What high school student or college literature major hasn't read his story "The Necklace"? (Well, maybe a few …) That tale, with a twist ending even the clever O. Henry couldn't top, is a memorably devastating piece of fiction.

But de Maupassant wrote hundreds of other stories and six novels. His last novel, *Alien Hearts*, is a mesmerizing tale of the relationship between an affluent young widow with many slavish male admirers and a man who cracks her coquettish-but-don't-fall-in-love attitude. The novel definitely makes one think of some novels the great Colette would go on to write.

Speaking of famous authors, Gustave Flaubert of *Madame Bovary* renown was de Maupassant's literary mentor. And de Maupassant was one of a number of high-profile French writers who was not a fan of the 1889-erected Eiffel Tower, even though he reportedly often ate in the restaurant there. Why dine at that locale? It was one of the few places in Paris where he didn't have to look at the tower!

Readers would not be disappointed if they looked at more of de Maupassant's work in addition to "The Necklace."

SHE HAD AN *INN* WITH A FAMOUS FILM DIRECTOR

I f film adaptations are any indication, **Daphne du Maurier** was one of Alfred Hitchcock's favorite writers.

Hitchcock made movies based on du Maurier's novels *Rebecca* and *Jamaica Inn* and her short story "The Birds." One du Maurier creation the director did *not* put on screen was *The House on the Strand*, a spooky and stellar 1969 book about a man who takes a drug to repeatedly visit the fourteenth-century past of the region he's living in during the twentieth century. There goes the neighborhood!

Given that the rotund Hitchcock made brief cameos in his films, it would have been cool to see him as a monk in the 1320s.

Hitchcock wasn't the only notable who comes to mind when thinking of the notable du Maurier (1907-1989). Her aunt, Sylvia Llewelyn Davies, was the mother of the boys who inspired J.M. Barrie's *Peter Pan* stories. And Daphne was the granddaughter of author/cartoonist George du Maurier, who created the manipulative and controlling character Svengali in the 1894 novel *Trilby*. Some people felt Hitchcock was Svengali-like when it came to treating some of the actresses in his films.

HER FAMILY WAS
QUITE A *GROUP*

Fame can run in families—but the high-profile people in **Mary McCarthy**'s family achieved renown in significantly different professions.

McCarthy (1912-1989) was the fiction and nonfiction writer remembered for her novel *The Group*, her political writing, and more. Her brother was Kevin McCarthy, the actor who appeared in movies that included the classic *Invasion of the Body Snatchers*. A distant cousin was politician Eugene McCarthy, who shared many of Mary's liberal views—including opposition to the Vietnam War.

Known as a critic as much as a novelist, McCarthy was *very* critical of writer Lillian Hellman—with whom she had a lengthy ideological feud. On *The Dick Cavett Show* in 1979, McCarthy memorably said that "every word [Hellman] writes is a lie, including 'and' and 'the.'" Hellman responded by filing a $2.5-million libel suit against McCarthy.

On a more positive note, McCarthy was close friends with political theorist Hannah Arendt and served as her literary executor.

Like many authors, the Seattle-born McCarthy was a person of more than one country—spending part of her time in a Paris apartment during the latter part of her life.

Mary was *not* related to Joseph McCarthy; she strongly opposed that politician's witch-hunt against supposed communists.

A LUNCH WITH ALL KINDS OF STAR POWER

One of the more intriguing gatherings of the twentieth century? In 1959, **Carson McCullers** (*The Heart Is a Lonely Hunter*) hosted a luncheon so that Isak Dinesen (*Out of Africa*) could meet actress Marilyn Monroe. Also in attendance was Monroe's husband, renowned playwright Arthur Miller (*Death of a Salesman*). The three women reportedly got along great.

Unfortunately, none survived another decade. McCullers (1917-1967) and Dinesen (1885-1962) had been in ill health for many years, and Monroe (1926-1962) would die of an overdose.

McCullers most famous novel—1940's *The Heart Is a Lonely Hunter*—was an amazingly accomplished book for a then-twenty-three-year-old author. Her other well-known works included *Reflections in a Golden Eye*, *The Member of the Wedding*, and *The Ballad of the Sad Café*. All skillfully depicted loneliness and other downbeat situations.

The Heart Is a Lonely Hunter and *Reflections in a Golden Eye* were both turned into movies (the latter starring Marlon Brando and Elizabeth Taylor), and *The Member of the Wedding* became a 1950-51 Broadway play (with Julie Harris and Ethel Waters) as successful as that 1959 luncheon.

A WHALE OF A DISAPPOINTMENT FOR AN AUTHOR

What all-time-great novel didn't even sell out its first printing of about 3,000 copies?

Believe it or not, *Moby-Dick* (1851), which also got less-than-stellar reviews.

The downward spiral continued for **Herman Melville** with *Pierre* (1852), which was lambasted by critics for being allegedly crazy, sick, perverted, etc. That odd novel focuses on a seemingly incestuous relationship and also has the title character obsessively write a badly received book—reflecting Melville's bitterness at the response to his wonderfully deep *Moby-Dick*. But the highly original, expertly written *Pierre* is also a masterpiece in its way.

Some 1850s critics should have been harpooned—metaphorically speaking.

The post-*Pierre* Melville (1819-1891) eventually lapsed into obscurity, writing poetry that didn't sell much and working as a customs inspector in New York City. A Melville revival in the 1920s (when the author's late-in-life *Billy Budd* was first published) started musician Moby's ancestor on his posthumous voyage to literary superstardom.

Melville also didn't live to see his Starbuck character in *Moby-Dick* inspire the name of a certain coffee chain.

A CAREER OF MANY SALES THAT STARTED WITH *TALES*

How's this for a literary debut? **James Michener**'s very first novel, *Tales of the South Pacific*, won the Pulitzer Prize for fiction!

But, in a way, Michener was hardly an overnight success. He was forty when *Tales* was published in 1947—two years after the end of the war that would provide much firsthand fodder for that episodic novel. Michener (1907-1997) held various U.S. Navy assignments during World War II.

As is well known, parts of *Tales* were adapted for the long-running Broadway musical *South Pacific*, which opened in 1949 and also inspired film versions in 1958 and 2001 (the latter for TV). The hit musical was ahead of its time in dealing with multicultural relationships; in fact, Michener's *Tales* novel was more cutting edge than readers might imagine when it came to depicting racial situations as well as the horrors of war, the boredom between those horrors, and other matters. (Michener's third wife was Japanese-American.)

Though his debut novel was published later in life than is the case with many other famous writers, the Pennsylvania-raised Michener more than made up for lost time. He wrote twenty-five more novels—many of them long, heavily researched, best-selling books. Among them: *Sayonara, Hawaii, Caravans, The Source,*

Centennial, Chesapeake, Space, Texas, Alaska, Caribbean, and *Mexico*. The much-traveled Michener also penned more than thirty nonfiction books, including the aptly named autobiography *The World Is My Home*.

A CONNECTICUT YANKEE IN LUCY MAUD'S COURT

L.M. Montgomery's marvelous *Anne of Green Gables* was published in 1908, and an avid fan of that debut novel was none other than Mark Twain. The elderly Twain said the whip-smart, redheaded orphan Anne was "the dearest and most moving and delightful child since the immortal Alice" of Wonderland fame.

Montgomery (1874-1942) would later create the equally delightful character of Valancy Stirling, the feisty young woman with allegedly only a few months to live in *The Blue Castle* (1926). Lucy Maud lamented that she never wrote what might be called The Great Canadian Novel, but *The Blue Castle* is certainly a wonderful work of fiction.

The Prince Edward Island-based Montgomery also authored a number of very nice *Anne of Green Gables* sequels, but the 1910-deceased Twain wasn't around for most of them.

HISTORY IS HER STORY, AND IT'S RIVETING

A mong the best war novels are *All Quiet on the Western Front, For Whom the Bell Tolls, The Red Badge of Courage*, and ... *History*.

If the last book doesn't sound familiar, you're not alone. *History* is magnificent and heartbreaking, yet it has only a fraction of the renown of the above-mentioned Remarque, Hemingway, and Stephen Crane works.

Why? Among the possible reasons: It was written by a woman— **Elsa Morante** (1912-1985). Also, it looks at World War II mostly through the experiences of civilians and has left-leaning sympathies (while essentially being skeptical of any governmental ideology). But if people avoid *History* for one or more of those reasons, they are missing out on a masterpiece—and several memorable characters.

One of them, Giuseppe, is among the most engaging kids in all of literature despite being conceived when a Nazi soldier rapes an Italian woman named Ida. The book also features two dogs and a cat with the most three-dimensional personalities you'll find in fictional quadrupeds.

Amid the characters and the story, Morante also starts each section of her 1974 book with a list of current events for the years Giuseppe, Ida, and other characters are living through. That fuses the personal with the historical, and certainly helps explain the novel's name.

Morante, an Italian author, knew the toll of war firsthand. In fact, she and her husband, Alberto Moravia (also a novelist), had to flee Rome for a year toward the end of WWII. And both were half-Jewish, like Ida.

FROM RUSSIA WITH LOVE OF LANGUAGE

Which author wrote his first nine novels in Russia but later penned his two most famous novels in English?

The answer is **Vladimir Nabokov** (1899-1977), who was born in St. Petersburg, spent fifteen adult years in Berlin, then moved to the United States, and finally lived in Switzerland.

Those two renowned books include the controversial *Lolita* (of course) and the somewhat-less-known *Pale Fire*—both of which are in various top-100-novels lists.

Pale Fire is one of literature's strangest creations. It includes a poem (by the fictional John Shade) followed by a long analysis of the poem (by the also-fictional Charles Kinbote) that's frequently hilarious and over-the-top. The perhaps-crazy Kinbote, who basically stalks Shade, uses his analysis to talk more about himself than about the poem.

It's a highly original novel filled with the wordplay and linguistic pyrotechnics at which Nabokov was adept. But the author was not adept at infusing much warmth into *Pale Fire*, which includes a murder depressingly inspired by the 1922 killing of Nabokov's father by a gunman targeting someone else.

Other interesting aspects of Nabokov's life include founding Wellesley College's Russian Department and, when later teaching at Cornell University, having future U.S. Supreme Court Justice Ruth Bader Ginsburg as a student.

A "GOOD" OUTPUT FOR A SHORT LIFE

T wo novels and thirty-two short stories are not a huge career output, but, then again, **Flannery O'Connor** lived only to the age of thirty-nine. Plus she wrote more than a hundred book reviews for Catholic newspapers, penned countless letters, and even did some cartooning (while in college).

Much of this output occurred while she suffered from lupus during the last twelve years of her life.

The Georgia-born O'Connor (1925-1964) is best known for her riveting 1953 story "A Good Man Is Hard to Find," which concludes with a cascade of violence yet also contains some dark humor. A lot of her work featured those two elements, as well as American South settings.

Oddly, O'Connor's first brush with fame came at the age of six when Pathé News filmed the future author with her trained chicken that did tricks such as walking backward. Later, the adult O'Connor raised dozens of birds—including exotic ones.

A good bird is hard to find? Not for O'Connor. Good stories weren't hard to find, either.

His Fans Rejoiced at His Partial Re-Joyce-ness

Brian O'Nolan (1911-1966) is not nearly as remembered as his fellow Irish author James Joyce, but the latter was an influence on the former when it came to a postmodern writing approach. Indeed, O'Nolan's *At Swim-Two-Birds*—whose characters rebel against their fictional author—was praised by Joyce near the end of Joyce's life.

Then there was O'Nolan's *The Third Policeman*, which features a story that's absurd, surreal, fractured, and darkly humorous. The novel—written in 1939 and 1940 under the alias Flann O'Brien—is almost impossible to summarize but it stars an amoral character who seemingly dies after helping to commit a murder and then meets various bicycle-obsessed cops in a strange netherworld. *The Third Policeman* is so weird that it wasn't published until 1967—a year after O'Nolan passed away. Being an alcoholic didn't help the author's relatively short life span.

O'Nolan was also a satirical columnist for the *Irish Times* and a government employee. One reason he worked as a civil servant was to help support his many brothers and sisters after their father's 1937 death. Having that job partly explains O'Nolan's use of various pseudonyms—which may also have something to do with the author being somewhat obscure today.

TWO DYSTOPIAN WRITERS IN THE SAME ROOM

George Orwell (1903-1950) is often coupled in the public mind with Aldous Huxley because they wrote the twentieth century's two most famous dystopian novels: Huxley's *Brave New World* (1931) and Orwell's *Nineteen Eighty-Four* (1949).

But there's another connection between the British authors that predates those iconic books by many years: Orwell (nee Eric Blair) was briefly one of Huxley's students when the latter taught at Eton!

Orwell was born in India and later served in the Indian Imperial Police as a young man before concentrating on writing. Not surprisingly, there were some struggles, including an early version of what became *Down and Out in Paris and London* being rejected by a publishing house's editorial director by the name of T.S. Eliot. *Down and Out* was eventually published elsewhere and became a success. It was for that nonfiction book that Blair changed his name to Orwell to mask from his family that he had lived as "tramp" when researching *Down and Out*.

Orwell became truly a best-selling author with *Animal Farm* in 1945 (the same year he may have been the first person to use the term "cold war"). *Nineteen Eighty-Four* would make an even bigger splash, but its author didn't have much time left to enjoy that success. The teacher (Huxley) outlived the student.

A BEQUEST FROM ONE OF HUMOR WRITING'S BEST

One of **Dorothy Parker**'s greatest accomplishments was revealed after her death.

Turns out that the legendary wit bequeathed her estate to the Reverend Dr. Martin Luther King, Jr. After King's 1968 assassination, the estate went to the NAACP, and, in 1988, Parker's ashes ended up in a memorial garden outside the NAACP's Baltimore headquarters. "Excuse my dust" was her proposed epitaph.

Parker (1893-1967)—New Jersey-born, New York City-raised, and a founder of the NYC-based Algonquin Round Table—is known for her one-liners, funny verse ("men seldom make passes at girls who wear glasses"), seriocomic short stories, screenplays, and, for *The New Yorker* magazine, "Constant Reader" book reviews. When assessing A.A. Milne's warm but cutesy *The House at Pooh Corner*, Parker famously quipped: "Tonstant Weader fwowed up."

Her best-known short stories included "Big Blonde" and "Horsie," and she co-wrote the screenplay for the 1937 version of *A Star Is Born*, featuring Janet Gaynor and Frederic March. That screenplay was nominated for an Academy Award.

Parker's gift to King didn't come totally out of the blue. She was involved in progressive causes much of her life—for instance, siding with the Loyalists during the Spanish Civil War and reporting on them for *The New Masses* magazine. Parker eventually ended up on the Hollywood blacklist during the McCarthy era.

A Government's Not-Noble Reaction to the Nobel

Which author received a Nobel Prize in Literature that couldn't be accepted until his son went to Sweden to receive it thirty-one years later? **Boris Pasternak** (1890-1960).

Pasternak was named to receive the 1958 Nobel for his sweeping *Doctor Zhivago* novel, which was initially published in Italy because Soviet Union publishers wouldn't touch it despite the (tentative) post-Stalin ideological thaw. The novel didn't fit the government's Marxist view, although Pasternak's book was more mixed about communism than against it—considering it somewhat positive in the ideal but not in the Soviet reality.

At first Pasternak gratefully accepted the Nobel, but pressure from Soviet leaders and many Soviet writers forced him to change his mind. The author feared for the safety of people close to him, and knew he might not be allowed to return to his beloved Russia if he left the country to receive the prize.

Pasternak died two years later.

In the 1950s United States—which had its own major human-rights issues with McCarthyism, racism, and more—the CIA used *Doctor Zhivago* as a propaganda tool because it felt the novel challenged Soviet orthodoxy and glorified individualism. The agency secretly had copies published and disseminated, even though it didn't own rights to the book.

Another fascinating fact about Pasternak: His artist father, Leonid, illustrated some of Leo Tolstoy's works and painted portraits of that legendary author!

SHORT LAST NAME, LONG FICTIONAL WORK

Edgar Allan Poe (1809-1849) is best known for his short stories and poems such as "The Raven," but he also wrote one novel: *The Narrative of Arthur Gordon Pym of Nantucket.*

While the length of that 1838 fictional work was a departure for Poe, the combination of sea scenario and horror was not. The author compellingly trod similar ground (similar water?) in stories such as "MS. Found in a Bottle" (1833) and "A Descent into the Maelstrom" (1841), but his *Pym* novel included an especially queasy ingredient: cannibalism.

Poe was also a pioneer in a couple of other genres: detective fiction (think "The Murders in the Rue Morgue") and time-travel fiction ("A Tale of the Ragged Mountains").

Another of *Pym*'s claims to fame is its possible influence on Herman Melville's *Moby-Dick*, which was published thirteen years later.

So when the greatest American authors of the nineteenth century are listed, Poe could plausibly join Melville, Nathaniel Hawthorne, and Mark Twain. Quoth the raven: "There are four."

BRITAIN'S BEST-SELLING AUTHOR OF THE 1990S

One distinctive thing about **Terry Pratchett**'s novels is that most have no chapters. It helps that his books—many of them comical fantasy works in the *Discworld* series—are so entertaining and well written that most readers don't really need the periodic visual break.

Pratchett (1948-2015) explained his unusual format by noting that life doesn't happen in regular chapters. But one unfortunate late chapter of his life involved dealing with early-onset Alzheimer's disease starting in 2007, when the British author had yet to reach sixty. Amazingly, the prodigiously productive Pratchett continued to write quite a bit after that—including five novels. One of them was 2009's delightful *Unseen Academicals*, in which the supposed-goblin-who's-actually-an-orc Mr. Nutt has some interesting memory issues that may have been influenced by Pratchett's condition.

The author donated about a million dollars to Alzheimer's research, participated in a BBC documentary series about the illness, and more.

How productive was Pratchett? He wrote forty-one *Discworld* novels during the thirty-two years between 1983 and 2015—obviously doing two during some years. His output also included sci-fi novels, graphic novels, children's books, short stories, maps, and more.

In fact, Pratchett was the United Kingdom's best-selling author of the 1990s. The man who didn't like chapters very much certainly never had to file for Chapter 11 bankruptcy …

FICTION HEAVYWEIGHTS KNOCKED OUT MENTIONS OF HER

Some books are known almost as much for what they influenced as for what they are in and of themselves.

That's the case with *The Mysteries of Udolpho*, a pioneering Gothic novel by **Ann Radcliffe** (1764-1823). The 1794 book is famous in its own right, but might be better known for being satirized by Jane Austen in *Northanger Abbey* (1817).

Also, Radcliffe's novel is directly referenced in works such as Sir Walter Scott's *Waverley*, Fyodor Dostoyevsky's *The Brothers Karamazov*, Henry James' *The Turn of the Screw*, and Herman Melville's *Billy Budd*.

Talk about widely known authors!

Radcliffe herself was a very private person. Her husband William often came home late from his journalism/editor work, and Ann began using that time to write.

Turned out she was a natural at penning the supernatural.

AN A-1 YA NOVEL THAT WAS MORE THAN A YA NOVEL

Which young-adult novel is perhaps the only one to win a Pulitzer Prize? *The Yearling* by **Marjorie Kinnan Rawlings** (1896-1953).

Actually, the compelling 1938 book is not entirely YA. Sure, it focuses on the preteen Jody Baxter and his relationship with an orphaned fawn, but it also focuses on Jody's parents and other adults in 1870s rural Florida and is filled with the harsh realities of life and death.

As a rural Floridian for part of her life, Rawlings knew that milieu, but not when she was Jody's age. The future author was born in Washington, D.C., attended college in Wisconsin, lived with her first husband in Kentucky and New York, and didn't move to The Sunshine State until an inheritance from her mother enabled her to buy land there in 1928.

The Yearling was made into a 1946 movie starring Gregory Peck and Jane Wyman as the Baxter parents. Decades later, in 1983, came the release of the *Cross Creek* film starring Mary Steenburgen that was based on Rawlings' memoir of the same name.

As is the case with many movies based on novels or memoirs, most of the actresses and actors in *The Yearling* and *Cross Creek* were more glamorous and better looking than the fictional characters or real people they played. But one *really* real person was in the latter film: Rawlings' second husband, Norton Baskin—who long outlived Marjorie—made a cameo appearance as an old man sitting in a rocking chair. Hardly a YA (young adult).

ALL NOT QUIET ON THE WEDDING FRONT

C harlie Chaplin made comedic movies and **Erich Maria Remarque**'s books were made into serious movies, but each shared a preference for PG. Why? Both were married to actress Paulette Goddard (at different times).

Actually, Chaplin and Goddard may have lived together rather than tied the knot, and it was rumored that this arrangement possibly helped cost Goddard the Scarlett O'Hara role that went to Vivien Leigh in 1939's *Gone with the Wind* (though Leigh and future husband Laurence Olivier weren't exactly sin-free: they were having an extramarital affair themselves around that time).

Goddard and the 1898-born Remarque—author of remarkable novels such as *All Quiet on the Western Front*, *Arch of Triumph*, and *The Night in Lisbon*—wed in 1958. The reportedly happy marriage ended when the man who also wrote *A Time to Love and a Time to Die* passed away in 1970.

Another author/Chaplin connection: **J.D. Salinger** (1919-2010) of *The Catcher in the Rye* fame dated playwright Eugene O'Neill's daughter Oona before Oona began seeing Chaplin, whom she ended up marrying.

APPRECIATING MORE THAN *THE APPRENTICESHIP*

We hear a lot of debate about what might be The Great American Novel, but what about The Great Canadian Novel? Certainly some books by Margaret Atwood are in the running, but a case could also be made for **Mordecai Richler**'s *Solomon Gursky Was Here.*

The 1989 multigenerational, nonlinear novel chronicles the memorable Gurskys (a Jewish family reportedly based on Canada's real-life Bronfmans of liquor-business fame) while referencing important events in the country's history and being periodically humorous.

Yet Richler (1931-2001) is better known for writing *The Apprenticeship of Duddy Kravitz* because that 1959 book became a successful 1974 film (starring Richard Dreyfuss as the title character).

In addition to his ten novels, Richler wrote short stories, the *Jacob Two-Two* children's books (later made into a TV series), travel books, essays, newspaper columns, magazine articles, and film scripts.

Richler was raised in Montreal, spent a couple years in Paris as a young adult, returned to Montreal, and then lived eighteen years in London—so he was also in the countries with candidates for The Great French Novel and The Great British Novel.

STRONG POISON AND STRONGER WRITING

Talk about being versed in the lower and higher arts—**Dorothy L. Sayers** (1893-1957) worked for a number of years at a London ad agency and also did a highly regarded translation of Dante's epic poem *The Divine Comedy* after teaching herself old Italian.

But Sayers is best known as a popular mystery writer whose often-seriocomic crime novels include those that star engaging amateur detective Lord Peter Wimsey. Several also feature brainy mystery writer (sound familiar?) Harriet Vane, who takes center stage in Sayers' feminist, women's-college-set *Gaudy Night* (1935). Peter had expressed interest in marrying Harriet the first time they met—while she was in prison, accused of murder, in *Strong Poison* (1930).

Sayers also wrote poetry, plays, religious books, and more.

The British author was good friends with C.S. Lewis, who was good friends with J.R.R. Tolkien, who wasn't a fan of some of Sayers' novels. No accounting for taste …

In one novel, Sayers combined her mystery and advertising talents. The title, not surprisingly: *Murder Must Advertise*.

To Sir with Love
of Anonymity

When *Waverley* was published in 1814, the author's name was nowhere to be found on the novel's front cover or inside pages.

Why did **Walter Scott** (1771-1832) choose anonymity? Part of the reason involved the fact that he was a renowned poet (*The Lay of the Last Minstrel, The Lady of the Lake,* etc.) at a time when poems were considered more prestigious than novels.

Even as *Waverley* and subsequent Scott books such as *Rob Roy* and *Ivanhoe* became immensely popular, Sir Walter kept up the anonymity—though his authorship of those novels eventually became an open secret among some of his friends and some of the public.

The Scottish author's most famous line ("*oh what a tangled web we weave/when first we practise to deceive*") is from his *Marmion* poem rather than any of his excellent novels. Some people erroneously think those immortal words were written by Shakespeare, who's far from anonymous in the canon of great literature.

HIS RÉSUMÉ INCLUDED A "THING TWO"

Theodor Seuss Geisel (aka **Dr. Seuss**) was a children's author extraordinaire, but did you know that he also worked briefly as a political cartoonist?

He drew for the left-leaning *PM* daily newspaper from 1941 to 1943—a two-year period that came after Geisel (1904-1991) started writing children's books but before he created iconic works such as *The Cat in the Hat* (1957).

Reportedly, the Uncle Sam in Geisel's political cartoons was a prototype for the hatted cat's physical appearance. Both have certainly made some mischief.

SHE CREATED A MONSTER AND A VARIED CAREER

Mary Shelley is known as the author of *Frankenstein* (penned when she was just twenty!), the wife of famous poet Percy Bysshe Shelley, and the daughter of also-famous writer/feminist Mary Wollstonecraft and philosopher William Godwin. But there was more to her life than that.

Shelley (1797-1851) authored a number of other fiction books (such as historical novels and the gripping apocalyptic tale *The Last Man*); did travel, biographical, and magazine writing; edited her husband's work; and espoused progressive views about feminism, political reform, and other matters.

Unfortunately, Shelley's life was also dogged by tragedy: the death of her mother just days after Mary was born, the 1822 drowning death of Percy Bysshe in a boating accident, and the early deaths of three of the four Shelley children.

The name of Mary's surviving child: Percy.

A MASTERPIECE FROM A MILLENNIUM AGO

Some people consider *Don Quixote* the first great modern novel, but a memorable novel preceded it by a few years—as in 600. That was *The Tale of Genji*, written by imperial lady-in-waiting **Murasaki Shikibu** (973?-1015?) of Japan. Her sometimes-absorbing, sometimes-boring, multi-character, chaptered book chronicles the life and loves of a charismatic emperor's son and depicts what happens with subsequent generations.

A 1985 edition of *Genji* translated and abridged by Edward G. Seidensticker quotes American-born Japanese scholar Donald Keene as saying that Shikibu's book is "the world's first real novel."

The original manuscript has been lost, but it was copied (and later translated) numerous times.

A woman writing a thousand years ago was certainly tilting at windmills; Shikibu did it successfully and for the ages.

ON THE AUTHOR OF
ON THE BEACH

Nevil Shute—best known for his post-apocalyptic novel *On the Beach*—was one of those people who used the proverbial "two sides of the brain." He was not only an author but an aeronautical engineer as well.

His "techie" side can be seen in a number of his approximately two dozen novels. For instance, *On the Beach* is a powerful, emotionally wrenching story of people in Australia living their lives in various ways as a wave of bombing-caused fatal radiation bears down on them from the north, but the book also tells us plenty about the workings of a submarine and even spends some pages on car racing—a hobby of Shute's in real life.

There were also two geographical sides of Shute (1899-1960). He was born in London and spent much of his life in England before moving in his later years to Australia (helping make that country's milieu ring true in *On the Beach*).

And there was even another side to the author's name—his full moniker was Nevil Shute Norway. He dropped "Norway" from his novels to protect his engineering career from any possible negative publicity from those works.

On the Beach received mostly positive reviews—even raves—though the U.S. government criticized it for depicting a nuclear holocaust that left no survivors. But one of the novel's strengths is its refusal to be optimistic about the human toll of massive radiation, even as Shute's book is optimistic about the goodness of many humans. Two sides there, too.

A Novelist's Political Race Lacked a Happy Ending

What do Ronald Reagan, Arnold Schwarzenegger, and **Upton Sinclair** have in common? They all ran for governor of California.

Sinclair, unlike those other two men, did not win his gubernatorial race—but he made a credible showing in 1934. Running as a Democrat, the left-leaning author received nearly 900,000 votes despite being red-baited by many of the Golden State's conservative politicians and media outlets.

The Maryland-born Sinclair (1878-1968) first achieved widespread fame with *The Jungle*, a muckraking 1906 novel that exposed horrendous conditions in the meat-packing industry. To help research the book, Sinclair spent nearly two months undercover at Chicago meat-packing plants. The book, which caused a huge drop in the sale of American meat, spurred new federal regulations the same year it was published.

Not surprisingly, Sinclair was a vegetarian for most of his long life. In 1967, less than a year before he died, the author was in the audience when President Johnson signed a meat-inspection bill and praised Sinclair.

Another Sinclair novel, *Dragon's Teeth*, won the 1943 Pulitzer Prize. And his 1927 novel *Oil!* inspired the 2007 film *There Will Be Blood* starring Daniel Day-Lewis. That movie gave the late Sinclair a California connection of a winning sort—receiving a couple of Oscars.

RABBINICAL RITES WERE NOT FOR THIS WRITER

Isaac Bashevis Singer's father was a rabbi, his mother was the daughter of a rabbi, and Isaac himself briefly studied to be a rabbi. But that religious profession wasn't for him—and readers were and are very glad he became a writer instead.

The Polish-born Singer (1902-1991) came to the U.S. in 1935, settled in New York City, and began penning stories and columns for *The Jewish Daily Forward*, which would also publish his fiction. Singer—who identified with Judaism but wasn't particularly observant—wrote only in Yiddish although he also spoke fluent Hebrew, Polish, and English.

His literary influences included the far-from-Yiddish works of Guy de Maupassant and Anton Chekhov. Like those French and Russian writers, Singer was best known for his compelling, emotionally complex short stories—including one, "Yentl, the Yeshiva Boy," made into the 1983 *Yentl* movie directed, co-written, and co-produced by Barbra Streisand, who starred as well. But Singer also authored nearly twenty novels, including *The Family Moskat* and *Enemies, a Love Story*—the latter made into a 1989 film.

The 1978 winner of the Nobel Prize in Literature was no enemy of animals: He turned vegetarian the last thirty-five years of his life. The author wrote that meat-eaters were, in a way, Nazis because "for the animals, it is an eternal Treblinka"—referring to the infamous extermination camp.

OF MOVIES AND MEN

By Joad ... uh ... Jove, were you aware that **John Steinbeck** (1902-1968) wrote screenplays that had nothing to do with his books?

One of his movie scripts was for Alfred Hitchcock's *Lifeboat* (1944) and another for Elia Kazan's *Viva Zapata!* (1952), starring Marlon Brando. Kazan also directed *East of Eden* (1955), the film version of the sprawling 1952 Steinbeck novel that many consider his second-best book after *The Grapes of Wrath*.

Kazan earned the wrath of many principled people when he "named names" during the McCarthy era, and Steinbeck left his progressive mental Eden late in life to support the Vietnam War. Two possible reasons for the liberal Steinbeck's seemingly surprising stance: he was friendly with President Johnson, and one of the author's sons was fighting in Southeast Asia.

That war was strongly opposed by actress Jane Fonda—daughter of the man (Henry Fonda) who superbly played Tom Joad in *The Grapes of Wrath* movie.

THE UNCONVENTIONAL LIFE OF A SINGLE-NAMED AUTHOR

There are several unusual things about **Stendhal** (1783-1842) and his career.

As a writer, Marie Henri Beyle used more than 200 pen names—including the Stendhal one that became his most famous. Reportedly, Beyle admired archaeologist/art historian Johann Joachim Winckelmann from the German city of Stendal.

(The one-word-nature of Beyle's alias also has the distinction of sounding quite modern; in recent decades, many celebrities have gone by a single moniker—such as the music world's Bono, Beyoncé, Adele, Madonna, Sting, and Cher.)

Another unusual thing about Stendhal's career is the way he wrote (after serving under Napoleon in various campaigns) a number of nonfiction books before turning to fiction. His two most famous novels would be *The Red and the Black* and *The Charterhouse of Parma*.

That second book also has its unusual aspects—written by a French author but set in Italy, and quite offbeat with its plot twists, mix of realism and melodrama, political intrigue, the shifting identity of its protagonist Fabrizio, etc. Plus Stendhal wrote the 500-plus-page novel in a frenzy of just fifty-two days.

Despite the speed of its writing, *The Charterhouse of Parma* received a rave review from Honoré de Balzac and was greatly admired by Henry James and Leo Tolstoy.

THE *STRANGE CASE* OF A FINAL *TREASURE*

Some authors save the best for last. **Robert Louis Stevenson** was one of them.

Stevenson (1850-1894) wrote several iconic novels, including the psychologically astute *Strange Case of Dr. Jekyll and Mr. Hyde* and the adventure tale *Treasure Island*. But neither had the depth, maturity, and rich writing of *Weir of Hermiston*, Stevenson's unfinished final work about a sensitive Scottish man estranged from his crude upper-class father. Archie Weir leaves home and is touchingly falling in love when the book ends (because of Stevenson's death).

Other authors—such as F. Scott Fitzgerald with *The Last Tycoon*—wrote unfinished final works that were quite absorbing but not their best fiction. Stevenson was an exception to that rule.

Coincidentally, both Stevenson and Fitzgerald died at the age of forty-four.

A RENAISSANCE MAN AMONG WRITERS

Who was the first non-European to win the Nobel Prize in Literature? The masterful Bengali writer **Rabindranath Tagore** (1861-1941).

Best known for his poetry and music (he composed more than 2,000 songs!), Tagore also penned novels, short stories, plays, essays, and travel pieces; painted; and directed a film. He even founded a university (Visva-Bharati) to put into practical form his disdain of rote learning.

Born to a prominent family in Calcutta (now Kolkata), Tagore would travel to more than thirty countries on five continents—where he gained the attention of many fellow writers and other famous figures such as Albert Einstein. Irish poet William Butler Yeats contributed the preface for an English translation of *Gitanjali*, though, unfortunately, the brilliance of that Tagore poetry collection and his other work was often partly lost when appearing in other languages. And Tagore—who opposed imperialism and supported Indian nationalism—influenced writers such as Chile's Pablo Neruda.

Sadly, Tagore's Nobel Prize was stolen from a vault at Visva-Bharati University in 2004. Later that year, the Swedish Academy presented two replicas to the university.

A Precocious Pair of Pulitzer Prizes

Who won two of the first four Pulitzer Prizes in the "Novel" category after that award began in 1917? Willa Cather? Sinclair Lewis? Upton Sinclair? Theodore Dreiser? Edith Wharton? Nope, it was **Booth Tarkington** (1869-1946).

The Indiana native received the prestigious literary honor for *The Magnificent Ambersons* in 1919 and *Alice Adams* in 1922. The only books breaking Tarkington's Pulitzer dominance were Ernest Poole's now-little-known *His Family* in 1918 and Wharton's enduring classic *The Age of Innocence* in 1921. (There were no 1917 or 1920 winners.)

Just two other authors—William Faulkner and John Updike—would later join Tarkington as two-time winners of a Pulitzer category that was renamed "Fiction" starting in 1948.

Tarkington's two honored books were both turned into well-known films. The 1935 *Alice Adams* movie starred Katharine Hepburn, and 1942's *The Magnificent Ambersons* was directed by Orson Welles.

Another Tarkington claim to fame was being pals with Woodrow Wilson; the future author met the future U.S. president at Princeton University in the 1890s. Woodrow was a Democrat and Booth a Republican, but they both held office. Tarkington was elected to one term in the Indiana House of Representatives in 1902—seventeen years before joining "the House of Pulitzers."

A WIN-WIN SITUATION FOR UNWIN

When British professor **J.R.R. Tolkien** wrote a story starring a hobbit, it was designed just for his children's pleasure. But luckily for the general public, the tale came to the attention of George Allen & Unwin—a publishing firm that released *The Hobbit* book in 1937. It quickly became a bestseller.

So Tolkien (1892-1973) was asked to write a sequel, but it took more than a decade to complete. That's because his follow-up effort was the epic trilogy *The Lord of the Rings*, a much deeper fantasy work than its delightful predecessor. Despite mixed reviews, the saga of Frodo and company was snapped up by many readers after its 1954-55 release.

Sales *really* skyrocketed after paperback editions of *The Lord of the Rings* came out a decade later. The then-retired Tolkien enjoyed the fame and fortune, but not the middle-of-the-night phone calls from American admirers or the gathering of Middle-earth fans outside his home hoping to see their *preciousss* author.

Given that those trilogy aficionados did not have the benefit of being the author's children, they sure were glad Tolkien's fiction writing got seen outside his home one fateful 1930s day.

LEO TOLSTOY, EARLY MOVIE STAR

Today, the iconic author **Leo Tolstoy** (1828-1910) seems to have lived so long ago that it's amazing to think that extensive film footage of his eightieth-birthday celebration exists. It can be seen on YouTube, as can Mark Twain footage I'll soon mention in another chapter.

Tolstoy—of noble birth but later democratic and even anarchist in his thinking—also has a modern sheen in the way his philosophy of nonviolent resistance influenced Gandhi (who corresponded with Tolstoy during the last year of the author's life) and the Reverend Dr. Martin Luther King, Jr.

The Russian author's writing was partly influenced by French author Victor Hugo, whom Tolstoy met during an early-1860s European trip. And Tolstoy's admirers—during and after his life—included Gustave Flaubert, Fyodor Dostoyevsky, Anton Chekhov, Virginia Woolf, and James Joyce. Chekhov visited Tolstoy a number of times.

Of course, Tolstoy is best known for his iconic novels *War and Peace* and *Anna Karenina*, as well as for short-story masterpieces like "The Death of Ivan Ilyich" and "The Kreutzer Sonata" (the latter is almost novella length). Nearly as long as *War and Peace* was the author's list of children: he had fourteen—one of whom lived until the not-so-long-ago year of 1979.

POSTHUMOUS PUBLICATION, POPULARITY, AND PULITZER

One of the most famous human-interest stories in modern literature is how *A Confederacy of Dunces* got published more than a decade after author **John Kennedy Toole** (1937-1969) committed suicide.

He took his life at least partly because his tragicomic novel was rejected—for reasons that probably ranged from publisher stupidity to the book being "politically incorrect" and having a rather unlikable protagonist (the gluttonous, chaos-wreaking Ignatius Reilly). It was Toole's mother, Thelma, who tirelessly worked to get *A Confederacy of Dunces* posthumously published—finally attracting the interest of novelist Walker Percy. (Interestingly, both Ignatius and Percy's *The Moviegoer* protagonist Binx Bolling were into films.) Louisiana State University Press released Toole's hilarious novel in 1980 and it won the Pulitzer Prize for fiction the following year.

In his *A Confederacy of Dunces* foreword, Percy recalled reading the pushed-on-him manuscript with "growing excitement … surely it was not possible it was so good." But it was. Yet it still took Percy several years to find a publisher that would take the book on. Perhaps one reason was that its vivid cast includes African-American, Latino, gay, and lesbian characters, along with the straight white ones. All that diversity certainly reflected the novel's New Orleans setting.

John Kennedy Toole wrote his first novel, *The Neon Bible*, as a teen. He later described it as not very good, but the fame for *A Confederacy of Dunces* led that early book to also be published posthumously.

REPORTS OF BEING NEIGHBORS WERE NOT EXAGGERATED

Did **Mark Twain** (1835-1910) ever borrow a cup of sugar from *Uncle Tom's Cabin* author **Harriet Beecher Stowe** (1811-1896)? Possibly, because they owned adjacent homes in the Nook Farm section of Hartford, Connecticut.

Twain lived in his huge Hartford mansion from 1874 to 1891, during which time he wrote his classic novels *The Adventures of Tom Sawyer*, *Adventures of Huckleberry Finn*, and *A Connecticut Yankee in King Arthur's Court*. Stowe's impressive home was also no cabin!

The Stowe and Twain dwellings remain today, and are open to the public. One highlight of a Twain tour is seeing 1909 film footage of the author shot in Connecticut by Thomas Edison's company. The clip can also be viewed on YouTube, but watch it in a well-ventilated room, because Twain is avidly smoking his ever-present cigar.

THE "FUNNY PAGE" ROAD NOT TAKEN

In 1990, the National Cartoonists Society honored ... **John Updike**? Yes, the novelist received the Amateur Cartoonist Extraordinary (ACE) award for having done some drawing before achieving fame in the literary world.

Indeed, Updike as a young man studied graphic art and wanted to become a professional cartoonist—long before Jim Davis created the "Garfield" comic strip starring a lasagna-eating cat.

Is doing a comic strip harder than writing books such as *Bech Is Back* and the saga starring selfish, sexist jerk Harry "Rabbit" Angstrom? Updike (1932-2009) seemed to think so. "A cartoonist needs seven ideas a week. As a novelist, I only need one idea every two years," he quipped at the 1990 ACE ceremony (which I attended) in New York City.

Who knows how literary and cartooning history would have changed if Updike had stuck to the drawing board and created a comic called ... um ... "Bech the Lasagna-Eating Rabbit"?

JOURNEY TO THE CENTER
OF HIS TALENT

Some great authors have little success with one kind of writing before finding the literary genre that best works for them. Such was the case with **Jules Verne** (1828-1905), who struggled as a playwright for several years before turning to novels. He then built a career that gave him the nickname of "The Father of Science Fiction"—with his most famous sci-fi adventure books including *Journey to the Center of the Earth, Around the World in Eighty Days, Twenty Thousand Leagues Under the Sea*, and *From the Earth to the Moon*. The French author—who also built a reputation as a writer of literary merit, not just popular renown—became one of the most translated writers of all time along with the likes of Shakespeare and Agatha Christie.

Another book by Verne was *Paris in the Twentieth Century*, but that prescient 1863 novel wasn't published at the time because of its pessimistic view of the future. It finally saw print well over a hundred years later—in 1994.

Verne, who knew Alexandre Dumas and worked on a play with Dumas' son, focused on more mundane concerns later in life when serving as a town councilor for fifteen years in Amiens, France.

AFTER BUYING A CAR FROM VONNEGUT, "SO IT GOES"

M any famous authors worked in other professions before (and sometimes after) they became successful writers. "So it goes"—or so it went—with **Kurt Vonnegut** (1922-2007).

At different points, Vonnegut did public relations for General Electric, opened a Saab auto dealership, and, in the unpaid arena, served as a volunteer firefighter.

But it was Vonnegut's deep experience with tragedy that directly or indirectly inspired his most memorable novels and the black humor in those books. For instance, his mother committed suicide, his sister died of cancer (Vonnegut adopted her children), and he was a German prisoner during World War II who survived the firebombing of Dresden and its civilians in an underground detention facility called "Slaughterhouse-Five." The name of that facility, of course, was immortalized as the title of Vonnegut's 1969 time-travel/sci-fi/antiwar classic—which features the melancholy catchphrase "So it goes," often after a gruesome death is mentioned.

Vonnegut wrote in an edition of *Slaughterhouse-Five*: "The Dresden atrocity ... was so meaningless, finally, that only one person on the entire planet got any benefit from it. I am that person. I wrote this book, which earned a lot of money for me and made my reputation, such as it is.

"One way or another, I got two or three dollars for every person killed. Some business I'm in."

ALL'S WELLS THAT ENDS UP WITH WELLES

H.G. Wells wrote the famous 1898 novel *The War of the Worlds*, which inspired Orson Welles' famous "The War of the Worlds" radio broadcast forty years later. Amazingly, H.G. (1866-1946) and the much-younger Orson both happened to be in San Antonio, Texas in 1940 and were invited to a joint radio appearance.

The two guests discussed Wells' novel and Welles' panic-inducing broadcast, of course, along with their similar names, the American psyche, Adolf Hitler, and more. Also, there was an allusion to Welles' then-upcoming *Citizen Kane* (1941) and how innovative that iconic movie would turn out to be.

While Wells wrote all kinds of books—including dozens of nonfiction works—the English author is best known for penning pioneering sci-fi classics that also included *The Time Machine, The Invisible Man, The Island of Doctor Moreau,* and *The First Men in the Moon.*

If you want to take a ride in a time machine yourself, you can listen to the Wells/Welles radio appearance on YouTube.

HER HOUSE OF BIRTH BEFORE *THE HOUSE OF MIRTH*

Edith Wharton's maiden name was Jones—a common moniker with an uncommon story attached to it. That's because the famous phrase "keeping up with the Joneses" may have started in connection with the wealthy family of Edith's father.

Wharton (1862-1937) certainly knew a lot about the lifestyles of the rich from personal experience—and used that knowledge to expertly tweak the upper classes in superb novels such as *The House of Mirth* and *The Age of Innocence* (the latter book made her the first woman to win the Pulitzer Prize for fiction). Ironically, the success of those two novels and many other Wharton works, including *The Custom of the Country* and her superb ghost stories, enabled her to amass quite a bit of her own wealth. But few would begrudge someone earning money by giving literary pleasure to millions of readers.

And Wharton often had sympathy for her books' less-affluent cast members, including the memorable Lily Bart in *Mirth* and the unhappily married title character in the riveting *Ethan Frome*.

Also unhappy was the Edith marriage that made her a Wharton instead of a Jones.

THE MEDIA OFFSPRING
OF *NATIVE SON*

Richard Wright (1908-1960) is best known for his riveting novel *Native Son*. What's less known is that the 1940 book had an interesting afterlife in other media.

Orson Welles directed a Broadway version of *Native Son* in 1941. Then, in 1950, there was an Argentinian film treatment of the novel—with Wright playing the teen protagonist Bigger Thomas despite the author being forty-two!

Wright moved from the U.S. to Paris in 1946, leaving behind a country whose racism he depicted so viscerally in much of his writing. Among his fellow expatriate friends was fellow famed author James Baldwin, but the two had a falling out when Baldwin wrote an essay calling Bigger Thomas stereotypical. Wright—also friends for years with acclaimed *Invisible Man* novelist Ralph Ellison (best man when Wright married his first wife in 1939)—felt that Bigger was representative of black males boxed in by a racist society.

NOVELIST'S MOST FAMOUS WORK MIGHT NOT BE A NOVEL

Was **Emile Zola** murdered? That question has troubled scholars and fans of a great nineteenth-century French author who didn't live far into the twentieth century.

Long before Zola (1840-1902) wrote the famous 1898 "J'Accuse" open letter that made him some serious enemies, he was famous for his many novels. Twenty of those books comprised the Rougon-Macquart series that traced the lives of two families whose members periodically appeared in more than one novel. Those R-M books often had specific themes as backdrops for the characters: *Germinal* and mining, *The Drinking Den* and alcoholism, *The Beast in Man* and trains, *Nana* and prostitution, *Ladies' Delight* and the rise of the department store, and *The Masterpiece* and art, to give a few examples. Speaking of art, Zola and renowned painter Paul Cézanne were childhood pals.

Zola wrote the "J'Accuse" letter—which appeared on the front page of the *L'Aurore* newspaper—that would eventually help exonerate falsely accused and convicted Jewish military officer Alfred Dreyfus of France. Zola's courageous stand in a case that reeked of anti-Semitism got him convicted of "criminal libel," which forced him to settle temporarily in England rather than face jail.

He did return to France, and died four years later of car-bon-monoxide poisoning from a stopped-up chimney. A tragic accident, or murder in retaliation for "J'Accuse"? The answer to that question has never been as clear as Zola's prose.

BONUS FOR READERS OF
FASCINATING FACTS!

Get ten more FREE mini-chapters with fascinating facts about ten
other famous authors. That's seven more mini-chapters than novelist
Alexandre Dumas had musketeers!
Download it here www.DaveAstorWrites.com/bonus

ABOUT THE AUTHOR

Laurel Cummins

D ave Astor blogs at DaveAstorOnLiterature.com, is the author of the memoir *Comic (and Column) Confessional*, serves as a National Society of Newspaper Columnists board member, and writes the weekly "Montclair-voyant" topical-humor column for Baristanet.com after having done that award-winning feature for *The Montclair* (N.J.) Times from 2003 to early 2017.

The Montclair resident is also a former magazine writer/editor, a former newspaper reporter, a former freelance cartoonist, a graduate of Rutgers and Northwestern universities, the husband of French professor Laurel Cummins (yes, she has taught literature!), and the father of Maggie and Maria.

Connect with Dave at www.DaveAstorOnLiterature.com and www.DaveAstorWrites.com

Printed in Great Britain
by Amazon